Claws & Jaws

30 New Zealand Animal Stories

Claws & Jaws
30 New Zealand Animal Stories

Edited by **Barbara Else**
Illustrations by **Philip Webb**

RANDOM HOUSE
NEW ZEALAND

National Library of New Zealand Cataloguing-in-Publication Data

Claws and jaws : 30 NZ animal stories / editor: Barbara Else;
illustrations: Philip Webb.
Includes index.
ISBN 1-86941-638-4
1. Children's stories, New Zealand. [1. Animals—Fiction. 2. Short
stories, New Zealand.] I. Else, Barbara. II. Webb, Philip.
NZ823.01089282-dc 22

A RANDOM HOUSE BOOK
published by
Random House New Zealand
18 Poland Road, Glenfield, Auckland, New Zealand
www.randomhouse.co.nz

First published 2004

ISBN 1 86941 638 4

Design: Kate Greenaway
Cover illustration: Philip Webb
Cover design: Katy Yiakmis
Printed in China

Contents

Introduction   9

1. The Korimako Kid   **Rachel Hayward**   13
2. Harry   **Margaret Beames**   20
3. Cat Attack   **Maria Gill**   25
4. Marry a Rat   **Lorraine Williams**   27
5. The Little Koura   **Debra Smallholme**   31
6. The Biggest Liar and Thief I've Ever Met
     Jack Lasenby   36
7. The Giant Weta Detective Agency
     James Norcliffe   43
8. Tui and the Pony   **Jane Buxton**   48
9. Pass It On   **David Hill**   54
10. Wild Tiger   **Bill Nagelkerke**   58
11. Henny Penny   **Janice Leitch**   62
12. Dinosaurs at the Deluxe Dog Motel
     Peter Friend   66
13. Wool You Join Us?   **David Hill**   72
14. Charley Two   **Lorraine Orman**   76
15. Bone Growing   **Janice Marriott**   81
16. Don't Feed the Keas   **Darlene Thomson**   86
17. The Weta in the Letterbox   **Wanda Cowley**   90
18. Bonecrusher   **Janice Leitch**   94
19. Mad About Elephants   **Margaret Beames**   99
20. Chirpy   **John Parker**   104
21. The Rat and the Little Black Scaup
     James Norcliffe   108

22. Fair Shares **David Hill**   113

23. The Scribbily Scrabbily Dinosaur
       Alan Bagnall   118

24. The Butterfly **Dianne Hogan**   121

25. The Last Horses **Jane Buxton**   126

26. Ms Winsley and the Incognito TV Star
       Barbara Else   130

27. Operation 'Dog' **Maria Gill**   136

28. A Tail in the Chimney **Rachel Hayward**   139

29. Winnie Weta's Scary Adventure with the
       Child-People **Jan Thorburn**   145

30. Scimitar Claws! **Jennifer Maxwell**   150

Acknowledgements   157
Index of Stories by Author   159

Introduction

Animals are all around us. Maybe you have a pet — a cat, dog, or cockatiel. Birds and insects live in your trees. Snails and worms work their slow way through the garden. A spider scurries over the lawn with its white laundry bag of eggs. Eels and ducks swim in a nearby stream. In New Zealand, even children who live in a city can easily see farm animals — sheep, cows, goats, and deer. Perhaps it is because we are surrounded by interesting creatures of all kinds that we enjoy reading — and writing — animal stories.

Choosing pieces for this book was great fun, but still difficult. New Zealand writers sent me nearly 200 tales about claws or jaws, tails, fur or feathers, fins or fangs. I wanted a variety of animals. I wanted stories that made me laugh, others to be serious or sad, some to make me think about imaginary places (like someone's dream-world about elephants), others to be about ordinary places like a kitchen, the countryside, a classroom.

One story came in an unusual way. A friend of mine emailed about something her little dog had done to help one of her neighbours. It sounded so funny that I emailed back at once: "Add a child into that story and rewrite it to about 800 words! I want it for my collection!" The result is the last tale in the book — a nearly-true story from Akaroa.

When I was at primary school I loved animals so much that I covered my room in pictures: bears, cats, horses, monkeys, dogs, and a poster of stampeding buffalo that made my mother shudder. I tried to count the animals in the stories I'd chosen for this book, but gave up and tried to count the pets I've had instead: one cat (Nakki), another cat (Fatcat), a dog (Tip), several budgies (very boring), two guinea pigs (who had many babies), another cat (whose name I have forgotten), a dog (Bingo), two white mice, three rabbits, more guinea pigs, hens, ducks (Honk and Ponk), a ram lamb, a black cat (Charlie), another black cat (Aubrey Strawberry), a black-and-white cat (Alcatraz), a tabby cat (Gretel) — oh, and once I had 17 slightly radioactive Texan salamanders.

My favourite real-life animals are cats. My favourite animal in this book? The toy tiger. Or the korimako — or the hedgehog — no, it's too hard to decide. And to choose my favourite picture in this book is impossible, because Philip Webb is so clever and funny with his illustrations.

As I said at the beginning of this, creatures of all kinds are all around us. Ideas for stories about them are forever hopping — flying — crawling — darting — swimming — leaping — past. I hope at least one animal in *Claws and Jaws* suits you.

Barbara Else

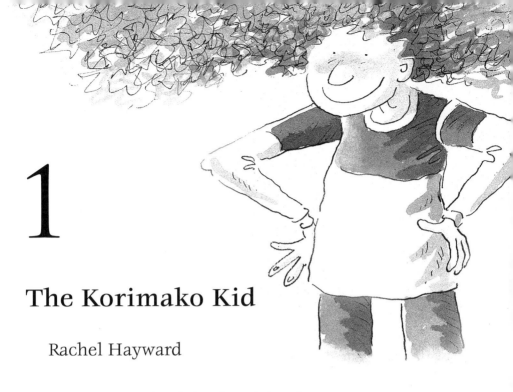

1

The Korimako Kid

Rachel Hayward

One morning, Ruby didn't brush her hair.

"Is this just a stage," asked her father, "or the end of hair-brushing altogether?"

"I'll let you know," said Ruby. By the end of the week, Ruby's hair was like a bush at the back of her head.

"It's a real bird's nest." Mum frowned and handed her a hairbrush. When Mum wasn't looking, Ruby dropped it in the bin. By the end of the month, her hair was a mad snarl of tufts and knots. "It's a new look," she told her parents.

"It's a shambles," said her father, smoothing his neat little beard. "You look like a hedge." But Ruby didn't care.

Her science teacher, Mr Garfield, took the class to Riverview Bird Sanctuary. Fantails flitted through the bush, tuis swooped and soared overhead.

"We're surrounded by the marvels of Mother Nature!" gushed Mr Garfield.

"Nature, schmature," grumbled Ruby, whose hair was caught in the branches of an overhanging tree.

That night, Ruby slept badly. Her dreams were full of rustling and whistling, fluttering and scratching.

In the morning, her brother Jason gaped at her across the table. "Ruby," he stammered, "your hair's a bird's nest!"

"Don't you start," Ruby snapped. A small cloud of feathers floated down into her cornflakes.

"Good grief!" exclaimed Dad. "He's right!"

Ruby rushed to the bathroom mirror and stared at her reflection. A pair of bright, beady eyes peered back. A greeny-brown bird was nestled deep in her tangled curls.

"There's a bird in my hair!" screamed Ruby.

The bird dug its claws into her scalp. "PEK-PEK-PEK!"

"Hold on!" said Dad, rummaging in the bookshelf. "What kind is it?" He pulled out a battered book, with *New Zealand Birds* written on the front.

"Who cares what kind it is?" yelled Ruby. "Get it out!" She ran shrieking up and down the hall, the bird squawking in her hair.

Dad handed the book to Jason and chased after Ruby. "Keep still so we can get a good look at it!"

"Here it is!" said Jason, peering at an illustration. "'Bellbird, or korimako. Dull olive-brown, blue sheen on the head. Lovely, liquid, bell-like song; alarm call a harsh pek-pek-pek.'"

"PEK-PEK-PEK!" shrilled the bellbird obligingly.

"What does it say about nests?" asked Dad, letting go of Ruby, who began jumping up and down, shaking her head.

"The nest is a cup of grasses, hidden deep in a shrub or small tree," read Jason. He looked at Ruby's bushy hair. "Well, that explains it. 'Nesting begins in September and lasts until . . . ' — uh-oh."

Ruby stopped jumping. She glared at Jason.

"Lasts until when?"

"January," said Jason.

Ruby fainted.

When she woke up, she was on the couch with her head propped on a pillow. Her parents were talking to a woman with a black bag. A doctor, thought Ruby, thank heavens.

"She's had a nasty fright, of course," said the doctor.

I sure have, thought Ruby.

"A good rest, and she'll be fine," continued the doctor. "She needs plenty of fluids."

Lemonade, thought Ruby happily. Ginger beer.

"Try some honeyed water in an eye-dropper," said the doctor.

Honeyed water? Ruby sat up indignantly.

"Lots of fruit too," said the doctor. "And insects. They love insects."

"What sort of a doctor are you?" demanded Ruby. "I'm not eating insects!"

"Not you, dear," said her mother. "The bellbird. And she's not a doctor — she's a vet."

As Dad let her out the front door, the vet called, "I'll be back in a few days to check on the eggs."

"Eggs?" wailed Ruby. "What eggs?"

"Be quiet!" said Mum. "You'll scare that poor bird to death. She's got three eggs to look after — she doesn't need you in hysterics every five minutes."

"Get this bird out of my hair!" ordered Ruby. The bellbird pecked her on the head. "Ow!"

"We can't," said Jason, waving the bird book. "Bellbirds are a protected species."

Dad came back with a net. "I'm off collecting bugs," he said. "Anyone else coming?"

Ruby spent an uncomfortable night, sitting up in bed so she didn't squash the eggs. She dozed until dawn, when the bellbird woke her with a long stream of flute-like notes, and lots of wing-flapping.

"A glorious dawn chorus!" sighed Mum, throwing open the curtains.

Dad came in with a tray. Ruby's mood lifted. Breakfast in bed was a treat.

"Honeyed water," said Dad, "gnats, fruit flies, and some kowhai flowers." He leaned over Ruby's head, and gave a warbling whistle. "Here, little korimako — keep your strength up."

School was a nightmare. The bellbird trilled loudly all through maths. Miss Powell, the music teacher, kept coming in to listen, and gaze at Ruby, her eyes glistening with tears. Mr Garfield sent his Year 8 biology class in to watch Ruby and make notes. The caretaker's cat stalked her all lunchtime, creeping up whenever she tried to sit down to eat her sandwiches.

"There's bird poo all over your shoulders," said Jason as they walked home after school.

"How long till the eggs hatch?" asked Ruby.

"Two weeks," said Jason. "Then two more before the babies leave the nest." He nudged Ruby. "Cheer up, Rubes. It's not all bad."

"What are the good bits?" asked Ruby, as they turned the corner. "Insect wings in my sandwiches? Feathers in my breakfast? Bird poo in my dinner? Is there anything I've missed?"

"Fame," said Jason, pointing down the street. Outside their house was a group of vans with satellite dishes, several camera crews and a crowd of reporters. Ruby gasped.

"There she is!" yelled a newsman. "It's the Korimako Kid! Hey, Ruby! What's the secret to your amazing success with native birds?"

Everybody raced up the road and swarmed around Ruby, waving microphones and shouting questions.

Ruby fluttered her eyelashes. The bellbird peeped out of her hair. "Patience," said Ruby, "kindness, and a true love of Mother Nature."

"Not to mention a really bad hairdo," whispered Jason. Ruby stepped on his toe.

"Any plans to save other endangered species? Kiwi? Kakapo?"

"Um, no," said Ruby. "Not at the moment. I'm deeply devoted to bellbirds."

Ruby was on the front page of every newspaper in the country. She was on National Radio, with the bellbird doing the bird call before the news. A natural history film crew followed her everywhere, waiting for the eggs to hatch. The Prime Minister gave her a medal for services to conservation.

Two weeks later, during social studies, Ruby felt a tremor run through her hair. There was a cracking sound from the nest. The camera man snoozing at the back of the classroom woke up and sprang into action.

All around New Zealand that night, people watched in amazement as three tiny bald birds hatched out of the eggs in Ruby's hair. Fragments of eggshell rained down onto her desk and she smiled her best television smile.

Just over a month after the bellbird arrived, Ruby's family drove to the Riverview Bird Sanctuary. They walked through the bush to a clump of kowhai trees, where the liquid chimes and clicks of bellbirds filled the air.

The fledglings in Ruby's hair flapped and cheeped. Their mother stretched her wings, and flew to a low branch nearby. She called a soft, sweet note to her babies. One by one, the fledglings crept from Ruby's hair, fluttered to the ground, and began to explore the bush floor.

"It seems no time since they were little eggs," sniffed

Mum. "And now they've flown the nest. You must be so proud, Ruby!"

"Whatever," said Ruby. "Now please, get me to the hairdresser."

In the car, Jason looked at Dad. "You haven't trimmed your beard since the bird arrived," he said. "It's getting a bit wild."

Ruby stared at Dad's curly, bushy beard.

"Is this just a stage," she asked, "or the end of beard trimming altogether?"

"It's a new look," Dad said, scratching at his chin.

Jason and Ruby exchanged glances.

"Hang on to that bird book," said Ruby. "I think we're going to need it!"

2

Harry

Margaret Beames

It was Gran who brought Harry home. "His owner's gone overseas," she said. "He needs a home."

"Mother," Dad said, trying not to sound exasperated, "you can't possibly keep even a small dog in your tiny flat, let alone a golden retriever."

"Well, I know that!" Gran said. "I thought you might take him."

Mum and Dad sighed. It was not the first time Gran had turned up with an animal she had rescued. Right now I can think of two cats, a rabbit, several hedgehogs and a duck. We had kept some until they recovered and found homes for others. There had been another dog, years ago. We'd kept her and when she eventually died of old age I missed her badly. I had asked again and again for another dog. But that had been before the accident. What use was a dog to me now? I looked at Gran suspiciously. Was this another plot to cheer me up? If so, it wasn't working. It just reminded me that I was stuck in this rotten wheelchair and would never be able to race around with a dog again.

But for once Gran wasn't thinking of me. She was gazing adoringly at the dog. "Look at him. He's so beautiful and so sad. All he wants is a family."

Harry lay on the floor, as flat as he could make himself, his head between his paws. He rolled his big brown eyes up at us and gave a deep sigh. He knew we were deciding his future. Of course we ended up keeping him. Perhaps it was those eyes!

No one asked me. If they had I'd have said, "No way!" The last thing I needed was a large energetic dog bouncing about all over the place.

The following afternoon, Gran popped in to see how Harry was settling down. I was watching some boring programme on television. Harry was lying by my chair with an expression of deep gloom on his face. That's all he'd done so far: lie around and sigh. Dad said he was missing his owner and we must try to cheer him up, but I wasn't very happy myself at the time.

Gran took one look at us and exclaimed, "What a picture of misery!" She's not the most tactful person in the world.

"Come on, we'll go for a walk," she said. She found Harry's lead and tossed it to me. "Put his lead on while I tell your mother we're going out," she said.

At the word *walk* Harry's ears had lifted, just a little. Now he came to me, fixing his eyes intently on my face. I leaned forward but I couldn't reach his collar.

"How can I put your lead on if I can't reach you?" I snapped at him, crossly.

Harry whined. He looked at me as if he was trying to work out what was wrong. He nudged the lead with his nose, then he put one big front paw on my lap. "Yeah right," I said, suddenly seeing how we could do it — and he must have got the idea at the same time because the next moment he had both paws sprawled across my lap and I was able to clip the lead to his collar with ease.

When Gran came back we were ready to go, and Harry was looking happy and alert for the first time. "You hold him while I push," Gran said.

Harry soon got used to the idea of trotting beside my chair. There was a park at the end of our street where we let him loose to run about and chase a ball that Gran had brought. He returned it to her time after time, never tiring of the game.

Suddenly he stopped, the ball in his mouth, his eyes gleaming. Then he dumped the ball in *my* lap. I grinned and threw it as far as I could. After that he brought it sometimes to Gran, sometimes to me. We never knew until the last minute which of us he would choose.

After that first walk, Mum and I had to take him every day. Around three o'clock he would appear by my chair, eyes shining, tail waving. If I ignored him, he would bring his lead and push it into my hand. If I was reading, he would nudge the book aside with his nose as if to say, "Come on, that's enough of that. Let's go!"

Another game Harry loved was tug-of-war. He was strong and could pull my chair the length of the garden. That gave Mum the idea of tying ropes to several cupboard handles, including the fridge. It didn't take Harry long to learn to pull them open so that I could reach in for his food and dish to feed him. Only once did he disgrace himself and steal food from the fridge! He was so ashamed when I scolded him that I felt terrible, and he never did it again.

Somewhere along the line he had become my dog. I hadn't wanted him, but he wanted me, it seemed. It was always me he came to for a game, his food, his walk, or just company. Dad made a bench for Harry to stand on while I gave him his daily brushing. At last Mum felt she could leave me while she went to the shops or had her hair done. He never went far from my side when she was out.

She was only next door when disaster struck, but still too far away for her to hear me call. What happened was this: I was watching television, went to change channels and dropped the remote control. "Darn it!" I muttered. I hated it when that happened. I had some long-handled tongs to pick things up with, but I'd left them in my bedroom. Rather than be bothered to go and fetch them, I decided to try to reach the box.

I leaned over, stretching as far as I could. I nearly got it, then — whoops! Over I went. Now I really was in trouble, stranded there on the floor with the chair on top of me. All I could do was wait until someone came. I was about ready to cry with frustration.

Harry came and licked my face. "Get off!" I yelled.

He wagged his tail. "It's not a game," I told him. "If you were as smart as Gran says, you'd go fetch help." I could see the phone on the coffee table, tantalisingly close.

Harry knew that word *fetch*. The trouble was he didn't know what to fetch. He brought me his squeaky duck first. Then he tried the cuddly rabbit he slept with. I could see I would soon be surrounded with toys.

"The phone! Fetch the phone!" I repeated. Harry watched my face intently. What was I looking at? Oh yes, it must be that black thing on the table. He sniffed it. "Yes! Fetch it, Harry. Good dog. Fetch!" At last he picked it up and dropped it by my hand. Saved! I would have hugged him if I hadn't been so busy dialling our neighbour's number.

The next time Gran came I showed her Harry's new trick. All I had to do was drop something beside my chair and he would pick it up and give it to me. "I'm going to teach him to fetch things by name," I said. "He knows *phone* already. You know, Gran, if you were trying to help me by bringing Harry — well, it worked."

"No," Gran said. "It was *you* who gave Harry the thing he needed most in all the world — a family. Now he's giving you his loyalty."

I reckon we're both pretty lucky, me and Harry.

3

Cat Attack

Maria Gill

Hissssssss, spit spit, meow! You are not touching me!
Hisssssss — I'll bite and scratch you — get your fingers
off! Swipe — I'll scratch anyone who comes near. Come on
— take me on!

Hisssssss, get that towel off me. I'll just get my paw
out — swipe! I scratch real good. So it takes four of you to
hold me down. I've had more. Yikes, the net. Get it off me!
Hissss, spit spit! You're not getting that mask on me —
hissss, spit spit!

Snooore!

Casey's eyes droop and her body goes limp; she is finally
ready for her small operation. She has been fighting another
cat and has a big sore on the side of her face. It makes the
left side look twice as big as the right. Dr Lamont wipes
the sore clean and snips at it with a pair of scissors. A
needle is then inserted into it and pus (horrible green stuff)

is drawn out. He wipes the area clean; her face now looks more normal and there is only a small pink hole left.

Dr Lamont notices that Casey has dirty and rotten back teeth. While she is still asleep, he opens her mouth and breaks the rotten bits off two teeth with a pair of pliers. He uses a drill to shape what is left of the teeth so that she can still chew her food. Another drill is used to clean her teeth.

The nurse comes along to check the heart monitor, which beeps every time her heart beats. She pats Casey and lifts up her paws. Casey's claws are very long and need cutting. Using the pliers, the nurse clips them back so they won't be so dangerous. Lastly, she cleans Casey's ears with a cotton bud.

Dr Lamont feels Casey's stomach to see if there are any bumps that shouldn't be there. He opens and checks her eyes, one at a time. The nurse disconnects the breathing equipment. Casey is lifted into her cage. She is much easier to handle while she is asleep. It won't be long before she is awake and hissing her greeting.

Hissss! I don't like it, I don't like it; whatever they've done. Meooow!

Oooh, my face doesn't hurt any more. Something's different in my mouth. Where are they? Now I can bite again. How dare they truss me up? Hisssss, spit spit!

4

Marry a Rat

Lorraine Williams

Mollie was using my skipping rope.

"Tinker, tailor, soldier, sailor, rich man, poor man —" she chanted, thumping down really hard and trying to make the old stone paving slabs wobble.

A few of the slabs were pink in colour, but most of them were grey. There were lots of crooked cracks running through them.

When it was my turn, I skipped really fast.

"Careful," said Mollie. "If you tread on a crack, you'll marry a rat. It's an old saying."

I didn't believe her. I skipped faster than I had ever skipped before in my life. Mollie began to cry.

"Stop! Stop!" she called out. She didn't want her best friend to marry a rat.

I couldn't stop skipping. The rope twirled faster and faster around me. The supermarket and the snack bar were just a blur. My feet edged closer to a l-o-n-g crack. I landed

— plop! — right in the middle of it.

My skipping slowed down to a halt. I stared at my feet. "Poof!" I said. "Girls don't marry rats."

A sleek black car pulled up beside us. A very elegant rat got out from it.

He was a jolly fellow, walking tall, with his tail thrown over one arm. A top hat was on his head and he carried a rolled-up umbrella. He pulled back the sleeve of his pinstriped jacket and looked at his watch.

"I'm not late, am I?" he asked. "When's our wedding?"

My mouth grew dry. I started to tremble. I didn't know what to say.

People tumbled through the doors of the supermarket. Captain Crayfish — from Captain Crayfish's Seafood Snack Bar — called out for everyone to come to the wedding.

I stamped my foot. I wasn't going to marry a rat!

"It's the law," said Rat. "If you tread on a crack, you'll marry a rat."

Everyone nodded in agreement.

Three bridesmaid rats got out of the car. Two of the supermarket shoppers started to sing 'Here comes the bride'. One small boy beat a toy drum.

"There can't be a wedding without a minister," said Mollie.

The rat was upset. "I'd forgotten that," he said.

Captain Crayfish pushed his way through the crowd. "A captain is allowed to conduct a marriage service," he said. He opened a book called *One-hundred-and-one Ways to Conduct a Marriage Service*.

"I won't marry a rat! I won't *marry* a rat! I WON'T MARRY A RAT!" I sat down in the gutter and howled like a baby.

"Yes, you will marry a rat! Yes, you will *marry* a rat! YES, YOU WILL MARRY A RAT!" shouted Rat. He jumped up and down, in excitement, on the stone slabs. His last jump was so high that it took him off a grey slab and

— plop! — onto a pink slab.

Mollie gave a scream. She pointed at the pink paving slab.

"If you tread on pink, you stink!" she crowed.

The rat looked taken aback.

"What's that awful smell?" said Captain Crayfish.

The three bridesmaid rats held their noses. "Rat, you stink!" they said.

Everyone agreed. "He's trodden on pink, he stinks," they said. "It's the law," they said.

Holding hankies to their faces, the supermarket customers and the snack-bar customers rushed away to finish their shopping.

Rat smelt like a bad fish. "Pooh," said Mollie.

"Oh dear, I think I'll go home and have a bath," said Rat.

He and the bridesmaids went off in their sleek black car. I picked up the skipping rope and began to skip.

I sang out, "Salt, mustard, vinegar, pepper —"

Mollie looked up at a cloud. "Ah-Ah-Ahhhh-CHOOOOOOO!"

It was raining pepper.

I shouted, "Quick! Ahhhhhh-choo-choo-choo! Let's get to — ah-choo! — school!"

I ran as fast as I could. I didn't stop once, not even when the skies opened and pepper thundered down over the entire town.

The Little Koura

Debra Smallholme

Tana lived with her dad beside the bush. The hills met the coast, and the sea sparkled blue or rumbled brown depending on the weather. Tana's favourite place was the creek at her Granny's house. The creek flowed from a freshwater spring and the water was so cold and clear that you could see every tiny drop of gold in the sand, shimmering in the speckled sunlight.

When Tana's friend Kim came they tore off into the bush, heading for the creek. "Let's hunt the mighty koura!" Kim called as she ran off up the path, past the old sheds and into the tangled undergrowth. They pushed the bushes to one side and found warm blackberries just waiting to be eaten. The trees became bigger and the branches higher, and soon Tana and Kim could stand tall on the stony path. The bush throbbed with insect sounds and life from rimu and rata, like the fat kereru pigeons swooping with their white chests ablaze.

The creek tinkled beside them, as it rippled over the stones and pebbles. The children lifted the wet stones, straddling separate flows of water with their bare feet, searching for the flicking tail of a koura. Freshwater crayfish, or koura, live in still, silent places, preferring the peace of the bush — unlike their saltwater cousins who live in the pulsing and pushing currents of the sea.

"This water is freezing," called Kim. Tana stood in it too, her feet looking large from above. She stood over the roundest stone and pushed it over. She saw the flick and flash in the shallows and pushed her hands quickly into the fine sand, grabbing a hard little body gently with her thumb and forefinger. If she wasn't fast enough, it would get away or nip her hand.

"Look!" she called to Kim. "Look, I've got one."

The native koura was about ten centimetres long, with a mottled brown-grey body and thick, grasping front claws. Under its long, curled tail lay lots of small red bubbles.

"What are those?" cried Kim.

"I think they might be eggs," said Tana.

Kim and Tana ran back down the sloping path with Tana carefully circling the koura's fat nippers, like a crab's, with her thumb and index finger, and watching for supplejack twines, which could trip her.

Dad lifted his protective mask and peered out from the dark shed.

"What's that?" he called out, above the sound of the welding machine, the dangerous white sparks showering his overalls.

32

"Dad," yelled Tana. "It's a girl. A koura, I mean. A girl koura with eggs."

"Well," Dad said thoughtfully, as he walked out into the sunlight, "I've got just the thing for that." He slid the koura into a glass jar, picked up a wooden box and some pliers, and headed off.

The children scrambled along behind him asking questions like "Where are we going?" and "What are we doing?" and "What are the pliers for?"

"Here!" Dad said, as he started to clip a long piece of finely meshed wire off the side of the old chook shed while the little koura waggled its legs.

"Just wait," Dad said, holding up his hand in anticipation of the next round of questions. "What we are doing is making her a home."

"Cool!" said Kim and Tana together, and they burst out laughing with excitement.

Dad asked them to hold the box, twist the mesh hard around it, and nail in sharp little tacks to keep the mesh in place.

They covered three sides, and then Dad carefully wrenched the plywood off the last side, leaving it to be covered with mesh only. Tana put five tacks and the small hammer in her pocket and they all headed back into the bush.

"Right, where did you find her?" asked Dad.

Up they went, past the sheds and supplejack, and into the tall trees. Along the path, where the gold flecks shimmered, to the biggest round stone. A little fantail followed them, diving and catching the insects they stirred up.

33

Kim laid the box in the creek.

"Put some rocks inside, Kim," said Dad. "That gives her some shelter during the day and will hold the box if the rain comes."

Tana carefully placed the koura in the box and Dad quickly pulled the mesh up over the last side. They bedded the box down into the sand and the water rippled across it. Kim nailed the tacks in, her tongue wedged between her teeth and lips.

The feisty koura crawled around and seemed not to even notice the box. There was constant fresh water, and a light layer of sand and leaves quickly washed in.

"How will it get food?" Tana asked.

"Little insects and leaves will wash in and keep her full," said Dad.

Kim and Tana spent hours checking the koura and

watching the box. If it rained they were anxious to know whether the creek was in flood and would remove or secure the box with more stones and rocks so that the little koura wasn't washed out to sea.

The eggs on the underside of the koura's body grew more and more red and full-looking.

One day they found that not all the eggs were

eggs any more. There in the box rambled a mother with tiny koura underneath her. The babies were making their homes in Granny's creek.

After a few weeks, Dad suggested that the best thing to do was to pull out the tacks and open the mesh, so that the koura family could leave.

"They can live on their own now," he said.

And they all agreed that the best thing of all was that, because of how they had treated the koura, there would always be koura to catch in Granny's creek.

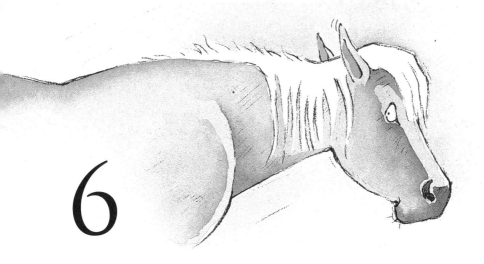

6

The Biggest Liar and Thief I've Ever Met

Jack Lasenby

When I reported at Ruatahuna, the field officer didn't have a mate for me. "I'm not supposed to let you go into the bush on your own," he said. "Besides, you look a bit young."

"I'm much older than I look," I told him.

"Why is your voice so high?"

"I'm not used to the cold up here."

"What if you get lost?" said the field officer. "I don't want to have to come looking for you."

"I never got lost in the bush out the back of home."

"Where's home?"

"Waharoa!"

"The Vast Untrodden Ureweras are a bit bigger than that hedge out the back of Waharoa," the field officer scoffed. "You'll be lost for months at a time. You'll be wretchedly lonely. You'll be so cold and hungry you'll wake up at night and cry for your mummy."

"I'm hiding from my mother," I said.

"If you cock up in the river, or fall off the mountain, I'm the one who'll have to fill in all the forms. It wouldn't look so bad if you had a mate."

"I'll be okay." I tried to look tough.

"I'll tell you what," said the field officer, "I'll let you take a pack-horse."

"A pack-horse?"

"You'll find a pack-horse better company than the average deer culler. He'll carry your pack, he'll never get lost in the bush, he'll chop your wood, light your fire, boil your billy, cook your tucker, and keep the camp clean. He won't pinch the best bunk and take the warmest place in front of the fire, and he never answers back. Gee," said the field officer, "I wish I was going to the lake with a pack-horse!"

"The lake?"

"You're going to shoot Lake Waikaremoana," said the field officer. "Here!" He pulled out a rusty Long Tom from under his house. "It's never been used so you'll need to work the bolt a bit before it'll shoot. A shot through it'll blow the mud out of the barrel. There's your rice, ten cases of condensed milk, tea leaves, sugar, and you can stick a handful of salt in your pocket. One tent, one camp oven, one axe, and one billy. Sign here! If you want more gear, you can scrounge it off the tourists up at the lake."

"I can't carry all that," I said, looking at the heavy cases of condensed milk.

"That's why you need a pack-horse." The field officer disappeared behind the stables and came back dragging something on the end of a rope.

"What's that?"

"Your pack-horse."

"What's he called?"

"Harry Wakatipu!"

Harry Wakatipu had large yellow teeth and snapped them when he heard his name. The field officer showed me how to put on the pack-saddle, adjust the breeching, the breast-plate, and crupper. The pack-horse bellowed and fought as I tightened the surcingle and threw a diamond hitch over the load just in case. I climbed on top, and Harry Wakatipu brayed and bit my leg.

"You've forgotten something." The field officer handed up my rifle. "You'll want these, too." He heaved up a heavy case of ammunition, and Harry Wakatipu grunted and bit me again.

"That blaze over there, that's the beginning of the track to Lake Waikaremoana. Build yourself a hut on the Hopuruahine River. Gee," the field officer said, "I wish I was going up the lake with Harry Wakatipu. In case I never see you again, good luck!"

He disappeared inside his warm house, and smoke poured from the chimney. It began to rain as we passed the blazed tree.

Out of sight of the field officer's house, the pack-horse bucked me off. When I came to, Harry Wakatipu was sitting on a log with his back legs crossed, rolling himself a smoke out of my tin of Pocket Edition. The pack-saddle and the load lay beside me. Harry Wakatipu struck a wax match on his rump and lit the cigarette, which stuck to his top lip as he stood on his hind legs, beat his chest with his front

38

hooves and said, "I'll fight you for who carries the gear!" I didn't want the field officer to find out I'd started causing trouble on my first day, so I put on the pack-saddle, and Harry Wakatipu loaded me.

"Keep up or you'll get lost," he said and galloped up the track. I followed his hoofmarks and the blazes.

Towards dark, I caught up with him. "Get the fire going, make us a mug of tea, throw up the tent, and cut some fern for a bed," said the pack-horse. "Pronto!" He sat in front of the fire while I put up the tent and spread his saddle-blanket on top of a heap of ferns. "Where's my mug of tea, gringo?" he shouted.

Now, you must let a pack-horse know who's boss at once or he'll make a nuisance of himself the rest of the time you spend together. I tipped a mug of tea out of the billy and handed it to Harry Wakatipu. He tossed it back and bit me.

"I take a big spoon of condensed milk," he said. "And a big spoon of sugar."

A weak man would have thrown it in his face. It takes a tough man to play the waiting game. I stirred in two big spoons of condensed milk and two of sugar.

Harry Wakatipu smacked his lips and drank it down. "Me and you are going to get on real good!" he said.

He let me drink the cold tea left in the billy before I boiled it full of rice with condensed milk and sugar for his dinner. All night I sat in the rain keeping the fire going, because Harry

Wakatipu said he'd bite me if I let it go out. He snored on his back in the tent.

Next morning the fire was going and the billy boiling when Harry Wakatipu got up and put on his saddle-blanket without having a wash. I had his tea ready with three big spoons of condensed milk and three of sugar.

"You make a fair sort of brew," said Harry Wakatipu. "Give us another!" I stirred in four spoons each of condensed milk and sugar.

Harry Wakatipu put the pack-saddle on me and galloped off without brushing his teeth. I had to pull down the tent, load myself, and follow. My plan was working even better than I expected. For two wet weeks I followed the old brute to Lake Waikaremoana. Every few hours, I found him waiting for me to boil the billy, and I put so much condensed milk and sugar in his tea, the spoon stood up in it. My plan was working.

At the bad ford above the Cascades on the Hopuruahine River, Harry Wakatipu made me give him a piggyback. Halfway across, I dropped him in. "I've a good mind to kick you into the Cascades!" he shouted and bit me. The field officer had warned me that nobody went down them and lived, so I swore I'd tripped. Harry Wakatipu didn't believe me, but he liked my tea. He led me down to where I was to build the Hopuruahine hut.

Before he would unload me, I had to light the fire and boil the billy. I stirred six spoons of condensed milk and six of sugar into his tea.

I was up all that first night at the Hopuruahine, making mug after mug of sweet tea for Harry Wakatipu.

He couldn't sleep because he had toothache.

As soon as I finished the hut he nicked the best bunk and pinched the warmest seat in front of the fire. He wouldn't cook, chop firewood, or sweep the hut. He wouldn't get up in the morning till I'd lit the fire. He grizzled about his toothache, answered me back, and sat around drinking mug after mug of sweet tea.

A couple of sacks of sugar and two cases of condensed milk later, all his big yellow teeth were rotten. He cried as I pulled them out with a pair of twenty-two-inch black-smith's tongs. I made him a set of false teeth out of green Plasticine. When he bit me, they bent. Now I was boss!

I was going to tell you that I always make Harry Wakatipu get up first and light the fire and boil the billy. I was going to tell you that I use him as a couch in front of the fire. I was going to tell you that I won't let him inside the hut even though there's a couple of spare bunks. But every word of this story is true, and the truth is that Harry Wakatipu won't do a hand's turn round the place. He's not just a liar, he's lazy as well. And he's a terrible thief.

While he still had his own teeth, he tried stealing my boots and, a couple of times, I caught him trying on my bush singlet. Nothing's safe from him, especially not condensed milk. I can't leave the tucker cupboard unlocked or else he's into it, swigging condensed milk straight out of the tin. And as for that field officer saying he'd carry my pack for me, Harry Wakatipu refuses to carry anything. He won't go out of sight of the hut, he's so scared of the bush.

"What was all that about carrying my pack and being my mate?" I asked him.

Harry Wakatipu sat in my chair, looked into the flames, and grinned.

"Here's your signature in the daybook where you swore to carry my pack."

"I never said I'd do anything like that," Harry Wakatipu said, grinning away to himself.

"Not only are you a liar," I told him, "you're a thief too! I saw you steal that tin of condensed milk out of the tucker cupboard."

"I did not," said Harry Wakatipu, still grinning away.

"You did so!"

"I did not!"

"You did so!" I told him. "I can see condensed milk every time you grin, all over your green Plasticine teeth." That took the grin off his face.

I'll tell you what: Harry Wakatipu's not just the biggest liar I've ever met, he's the biggest thief as well! He's dirty, he's always looking at his reflection in the river, and he's a coward. I'm sure you wouldn't like him.

7

The Giant Weta Detective Agency

James Norcliffe

There were dark jagged shapes all around me in the bush that night. Things made those strange chirrup-chirrup noises that chirrup-chirrup noise-making things make.

Scary things.

Not that I was especially scared. When you're in the detective business, you learn to be brave. And I'm learning. To tell you the truth, I tend to scare people more than they scare me. That's one advantage of being a giant weta. All the same, I admit I'm not the prettiest bean in the can. Nor am I the sharpest knife in the drawer. I should have realised that when I took on this huhu grub case.

Not that Hilda had been put off by my appearance when she turned up in my office that afternoon. She was one cute little grub. A huhu grub. An upset huhu grub. A sort of boo-hoo huhu grub.

"My sister's missing," she sobbed.

"Your sister?"

"Helga . . ."

"Helga? Right. What does she look like?"

Hilda dabbed at her eyes with a grubby handkerchief. "Oh, you know, Mr Weta. A segmented body, a little on the plump side, and sort of creamy white. Rather like me, actually."

"Got you. Very pretty."

Hilda blushed. "If you say so."

"Tell me about her. When did she go missing?"

I didn't want to upset Hilda, but I had heard that a number of huhu grubs had gone missing in the last few days. I suspected foul play — or rather fowl play. Probably a weka or a kaka.

"It was three weeks ago. I'd crawled off into my tunnel and Helga crawled off into her tunnel. We shouted 'Good night!'" Hilda sobbed again. "That was the last thing I shouted at her. In the morning she had gone . . ." More sobs. "All she'd left behind was one large, shiny suitcase."

Something did not compute. "Why on earth did she leave her suitcase if she'd gone?" I asked. "Why didn't she take it with her?"

"I don't know," wailed Hilda. "That's why I'm asking you!"

I'm a feeling sort of a guy — with feelers like mine I couldn't be anything else — and I couldn't bear the sight of her tear-stained face.

"Look, kid," I said. "I'll check it out. No promises, mind."

So now I was staking out the old kahikatea log that Hilda and Helga and all their other sisters had been chewing through since they'd been tiny. That evening I'd

44

seen her home, told her to stay put until morning, and looked for a spot where I could see anything that might take place. Any hungry kaka with a taste for huhu grubs would probably consider a giant weta an interesting dessert. So I half-buried myself under a pile of skeleton leaves and sphagnum moss.

The night passed slowly. High above, the wind moaned. There were chirrup-chirrup noises, and chitter-chitter-chitter noises, and once or twice a distant, unnerving shriek.

The minutes crept slowly by.

I began to think of all the reasons Helga could have disappeared. Every reason was pretty depressing. Of course, she could have just gone for a walk and got lost. But huhu grubs rarely leave the safety of their crumby crumbly homes. What had happened to her was more likely to have been along the lines of my first fearful thought: fowl play. It could have been a weka. Or that kaka. The sudden flurry of a morepork. Snatch. Gobble. It didn't seem hopeful at all. Huhu grubs didn't have much of a chance in the big, bad world. Bad things tended to happen to you if you were fat and slow and tasted, by all accounts, rather like peanut butter.

In the strange half-darkness before dawn, I became aware that I wasn't the only one staking out the kahikatea log. To the left I saw a slight movement. A leaf. A large leaf. There was no wind at all now, but the leaf was trembling and moving. It was moving slowly towards the log.

I froze. This was no weka or kaka.

Carefully, I shrugged off my cover of moss and began to circle behind the leaf. It was lighter now. I saw that the leaf had legs. Something was trying to disguise itself.

Could this be the clue I'd been looking for? Could this be the killer?

I allowed the leaf to move closer to the log. I followed at a safe distance. The disguised creature lifted itself onto the log and began trundling towards a large hole.

The same hole Hilda had disappeared into before I began my stakeout.

I crept closer. I heard a thin, reedy voice calling. Calling a name into the hole.

"Hilda!" it cried. "Hilda, come out!"

I was overtaken by anger. So this was how it happened! The killer called the name of his victim and the unknowing grub would come to the surface and then . . . This was what had happened to Helga, and, unless I acted quickly, this was what would happen to Hilda.

I seized the leaf and whipped it off the creature.

"Just one moment, buster," I snarled. "I'd like to have a word with you!"

Under the leaf was a long, thin beetle with a mottled brown back. It looked at me, startled and frightened.

"I know what you're up to," I snarled again. "What have you done with Helga?"

"Please!" the beetle quavered. "Don't hurt me!"

"That's rich!" I rose on my back legs and lifted the quivering beetle with my forelegs. "After what you did to Helga!"

"Put me down!" the beetle shrieked. "I didn't do anything to Helga!"

"Prove it!" I demanded.

"Hilda! Hilda! Save me!" shrieked the beetle.

There was movement at the entrance to Hilda's hole. Two large feelers came out, followed by a long, narrow body. A mottled brown body. A beetle, just like the one I was gripping with my forelegs.

"Helga!" cried the second beetle.

"Hilda!" cried the first beetle.

"What's going on?" I demanded. I dropped the beetle, who scurried to the second beetle's side. They waved their feelers at me soothingly.

"Mr Weta! Mr Weta! We're beetles!" they said.

"I can see that. So what's going on?"

"Huhu beetles!" they said. Then one said, "I'm Hilda" and the other said, "I'm Helga."

"Oh," I said. They were right. They were huhu beetles. Particularly ugly ones as well.

There didn't seem to be anything left to discuss, so I said, "Well, I'm off to my bed. There'll be a bill in the mail. That was one long cold night."

As I said, I'm not the sharpest knife in the drawer. I should have known when I took on the huhu grub case that there would turn out to be two huhu grub cases: shiny ones, each one shed and discarded somewhere in the tunnels of an old kahikatea log.

8

Tui and the Pony

Jane Buxton

Tui sat on the gate and looked longingly at Tony Scott's little grey pony. She would love to have a pony like that.

It wasn't fair. Tony Scott had every single thing in the world that he wanted. He didn't even have to want it very much. He was given something new nearly every week.

The pony looked small and lonely in its big paddock of long, lush grass.

Tui called out, "Come on! Here, pony!" and held out her apple core.

The pony limped towards her. "What's the matter?" said Tui. "Are your feet sore?" She jumped off the gate into the paddock.

The pony's feet were long and starting to curl up at the toes. "Poor thing," said Tui. "Your hooves need cutting. And you're far too fat." He looked sad and uncomfortable.

Tui worried about him all the way home.

"That pony of Tony Scott's, Mum, there's something

the matter with him," she announced as she walked in.

"That's a problem, then," said Mum. "The Scotts are away on holiday. I don't think anyone is looking after their pony."

"Come and have a look at him," said Tui. "You know about horses."

So Mum put the twins in their pushchair and walked up the road to the paddock.

The pony was standing by the gate. Mum took one look and said, "Oh dear. He's foundered."

"What does that mean?" asked Tui.

"Ponies get this way when they have too much grass to eat," explained Mum. "They get very fat. Their feet get hot and sore. If they're left for too long, they can die."

The pony pushed his soft grey nose against Tui's arm. "We must do something," Tui said. "We can't let him die."

"He needs a vet," said Mum. "And we can't call the vet for someone else's pony."

"Why can't we?" asked Tui.

"It costs a lot of money to get the vet out to a sick animal," said Mum. "The Scotts may not want to pay the vet's bill."

"I'll pay for the vet to come," said Tui. "I'll use the money I've been saving to buy a pony with."

Mum sighed. "It's not just that," she said. "We don't know the Scotts very well. They might not like us to interfere."

"But *Mum*!" said Tui. "The pony might die if we don't interfere."

Mum just sighed again.

They walked back up the road together. The twins gurgled happily in their pushchair. But Tui was quiet, because she could see Mum was thinking things over.

By the time they reached home Mum had made up her mind. "All right, Tui. I'll phone the vet."

Tui was waiting at the paddock when the vet came.

"This pony has foundered," he said. "Just as well you called me. I'm going to give him an injection and then I'm going to trim his hooves. Hold his head for me, please."

Tui held the pony. He didn't seem to mind the injection and he stood quite still to have his hooves trimmed.

"Good boy," said the vet when he had finished. "Now, young lady." He turned to Tui. "I've done my bit. The rest of the treatment is up to you. You must keep him in a stable, or a small yard with no grass. Just give him water and hay. It will help if you hose his feet every day, or stand him in a river to cool them down. You should take him out for walks too. No riding though; not for a while. It'll be a long time before he's well again."

"He's not mine," said Tui.

"I know," said the vet. "Your mother told me the whole story. Those people should thank you for saving their pony."

Just then a car pulled up with a shiny, new BMX bike on the roof rack. It was Mr Scott and Tony, back from their holiday.

"What's going on here?" boomed Mr Scott.

"That's my pony!" Tony cried. "What are you doing?"

"Your pony has foundered," said the vet, and he

explained to the Scotts what he had done.

"So now I have a big bill to pay, I suppose," grumbled Mr Scott.

"And I don't even want Billy any more," said Tony. "I want to sell him. My scooter is much more fun."

Mr Scott frowned. "Only a few months ago you wanted a pony more than anything else in the world, and now you want to sell him. That's just not on, son. And anyway, he helps to keep down the grass in the paddock."

"There's too much grass for one little pony," said the vet crossly. "People shouldn't keep ponies unless they know how to look after them."

"I know, I know," grumbled Mr Scott. "But now what am I going to do? I can't look after him myself — I'm a busy man. I could try to sell him, but no one would want a sick pony." He sighed. "Perhaps it would be better if he were put to sleep."

"Oh, no!" cried Tui. "*Please* don't let him be put to sleep."

"See, Dad," said Tony, looking at her. "This girl would buy Billy. You can see she likes him. Then I would have the money to buy a new trampoline. I really *need* a trampoline, Dad." He turned to Tui again. "You would like to buy Billy, wouldn't you?"

Tui didn't know what to say. Of course she'd like to buy Billy, but she had nowhere near enough money saved up. She felt them all looking at her, waiting for an answer. She hung her head.

The vet looked from one face to another and then at Billy, who was rubbing his head against Tui's shoulder. He cleared his throat and said to Tony, "Well, if you don't mind my saying so, young man, this pony is not worth anything now, except as dog tucker. He is certainly not worth the price of a trampoline. If the little girl would pay you dog-meat price — about fifty dollars I think, for an animal of this size — then that would pay my fee and the pony would be off your hands."

"Fifty dollars isn't enough!" Tony protested.

"That'll do, son," said his father gruffly.

The vet winked at Tui. "What do you say, young lady? Can you afford fifty dollars?"

Tui nodded her head. She still couldn't say anything. It all seemed like a dream.

"That's all settled then," said Mr Scott, and he shook Tui's hand solemnly.

"What's all settled?" said a voice behind them. And there was Mum, with the twins in the pushchair.

"I've just sold your daughter a pony," said Mr Scott.

Mum looked startled.

The vet smiled at her and said, "Your daughter just bought Billy for fifty dollars. I hope you won't mind. There's a lot of work in looking after a sick animal."

Tui looked up anxiously, but Mum seemed pleased. "Tui's very keen," she said. "And I'll help her. Are you going to come and live in our orchard, Billy?" She leaned over the gate and patted him.

The vet said, "I've told Tui the treatment Billy needs for the next few months. I'll call in every now and then and see how he's getting on."

Tui led Billy limping along the road to his new home. Tony biked with them to get the fifty dollars. He swerved and skidded in front of Billy, showing off his new bike. "Dad paid five hundred for that pony," he complained. "You should give me more than fifty dollars. But I suppose it *is* a lame horse. You should get a bike like mine. They never go lame."

"Just watch out you don't get a flat tyre, then," said Tui.

"Huh!" snorted Tony. "The bike shop could fix that in a minute. But Billy's going to take half a *year* to fix. And I will get a trampoline anyway. I always get what I want in the end."

Tui said nothing. She felt sorry for Tony, always getting what he wanted and then finding it wasn't what he wanted after all. Tui knew what *she* wanted, and now she had it. She smiled at Billy and patted his neck. For Tui he was a dream come true.

9

Pass It On

David Hill

It was a quiet morning on Ridge Street. Most of the humans were at work or at school. Most of the dogs were asleep.

At Number 7 Ridge Street, Baldy the Beagle lay on the front porch, in the sun. Suddenly his eyes blinked open. He'd heard something. What? Where? Who? Baldy lifted his head. There it was again — a noise down on the footpath.

Miaoww! Miaoww! A tiny grey cat was trying to duck down the street.

Baldy jumped off the porch. ZOOOM! He tore down the path. SPROING! He slid into the wire front gate.

"Woof! Woof!" barked Baldy. "A tiny grey cat is trying to duck down the street. Pass it on! Woof! Woof!"

Along the road at Number 9 Ridge Street, Raja the Rottweiler heard Baldy barking. Raja leaped up in her kennel. THWACK! She hit her head on the kennel doorway.

"Aarrff! Aarrff!" bellowed Raja. "A message from Baldy.

A tiny grey RAT is trying to duck down the street. Pass it on! Aarrff! Aarrff!"

Further along the road at Number 11 Ridge Street, Garbage Guts the Mongrel heard Raja bellowing. Garbage Guts jumped out of the rubbish bin he was searching through. KRANGGG! He knocked the rubbish bin over.

"Rruff! Rruff!" yelled Garbage Guts. "A message from Raja. A MIGHTY grey RAT is trying to duck down the street. Pass it on! Rruff! Rruff!"

Still further along the road at Number 13, Buttercup the Bulldog heard Garbage Guts yelling. She jerked up and fell off her chair. SPLASH! She landed on her water bowl.

"Grrr! Grrr!" grunted Buttercup. "A message from Garbage Guts. A MIGHTY GREAT RAT is trying to duck down the street. Pass it on! Grrr! Grrr!"

Across the road at Number 12 Ridge Street, Fang the Poodle heard Buttercup grunting. Fang sprang up from the carpet. CLACK! He knocked his owner's morning cup of tea onto the cushions.

"Yip! Yip!" yapped Fang. "A message from Buttercup. A MIGHTY GREAT RAT IS DRIVING a duck down the street. Pass it on! Yip! Yip!"

Back further along the road at Number 8 Ridge Street, Duchess the Doberman heard Fang yapping. Duchess sprang to her feet, gripping her breakfast bone in her mouth. WHIZZ! She sent the bone flying. SMACK! The bone hit her owner and almost knocked him flying.

"Bayy! Bayy!" boomed Duchess. "A message from Fang. A MIGHTY GREAT RAT IS DRIVING A TRUCK down the street. Pass it on! Bayy! Bayy!"

Straight across from Number 8 Ridge Street was Number 7. Number 7 Ridge Street, where Baldy the Beagle had seen a tiny grey cat trying to duck down the street.

Baldy was just trotting back to lie down on his sunny front porch again. Then he heard Duchess booming.

Baldy stopped and listened. ZOOOM! He tore down the path again. SPROING! He slid into the wire front gate again.

"Woof! Woof!" barked Baldy. "A message from Duchess. A MIGHTY GREAT RAT IS DRIVING A TRUCK DOWN TO EAT! Oh no, he's going to eat US! Hide, everyone. Pass it on! Hide!"

WHIZZ! Baldy the Beagle rushed away and hid under the porch at Number 7.

ZIPP! Raja the Rottweiler bounded away and hid inside the garage at Number 9.

WHOOSH! Garbage Guts the Mongrel raced away and hid behind the trash can at Number 11.

SPLOSSH! Buttercup the Bulldog hurtled away and tried to hide inside her water bowl at Number 13.

FLASHH! Fang the Poodle scampered away and hid under the cushions at Number 12.

KERTHUMMPP! Duchess the Doberman galloped away and tried to hide behind her owner at Number 8.

Everything was quiet and still again on Ridge Street. The dogs didn't move. Nothing else moved.

At last, Baldy the Beagle poked his head out from under the porch of Number 7. He looked around. He couldn't hear anything. He couldn't see anything.

Baldy crawled carefully out and lay down on the front porch again. He sighed a deep sigh.

Suddenly his eyes blinked open once more. There it was, down on the footpath. A tiny grey cat was trying to duck BACK UP the street.

10

Wild Tiger

Bill Nagelkerke

I'm sitting up in bed, making a raft out of the thin twigs I've collected from the creek bank.

Tiger lies on the bed beside me, smiling his lopsided smile. Tiger's my favourite toy. We've been together since we were babies. I've grown a lot since then, but Tiger's stayed small.

I hold him up so he can see out of the window. My bed overlooks the hospital grounds where the creek runs through.

I'm here because I've got cancer. Everyone wants me to get better and I probably will but there's always a chance that I won't. It's still too early to tell.

At the moment I feel pretty weak, although not as bad as sometimes. When I have tests and needles Mum or Dad usually stays with me overnight, but I've told them I can manage without them this time.

Besides, I still have Tiger with me.

58

Yesterday Frank, who's one of the hospital orderlies, took me down for a spin in my wheelchair. He helped me collect the twigs for the raft.

I'm just remembering that, when Frank comes into the room.

"Want to go for another ride," he asks, "or wait for your folks to arrive and take you instead?"

"I'd like to go now," I say. "What do you think, Tiger?"

"I'd like another breath of fresh air," Tiger says.

"He's really a wild tiger," I explain to Frank. "He belongs in the wild outdoors."

Frank wheels us along the corridor. We plummet down in the lift, and go outside.

"That's better," says Tiger. "I hate the hospital smell."

"So do I," I say.

"Where to?" Frank asks. "Let me guess. Along the creek path again?"

"Yes, thanks. I've got to get a few more twigs to finish the raft."

"It's coming along nicely," Frank says, picking it up and looking at it from all sides. "It should float really well."

"Will it get far before it breaks up?" I ask, trying not to sound anxious.

"All the way to the river and then to the sea with any luck. Is that far enough for you?"

I nod, even though I don't want my raft to go as far as the sea.

"Bit small for you," says Frank.

"It's not *for* me."

"Didn't think it was."

59

"I didn't think it was for *anybody*," Tiger says to me as I search the creek bank for twigs.

"There's a good one," I say.

Frank pauses so I can bend down to pick it up. I quickly weave it into the gap.

Tiger doesn't like being ignored. "I thought it was just something you were making," he says.

So I say to him: "I haven't told you yet, Tiger, but this raft's for you. And I think today's the day."

"For me!" says Tiger. "Today! I don't want to go anywhere in a raft. Not today. Not any day. Not without you."

"Listen," I explain in my most serious voice. "It's like I've already told you. I might get better, but I might not. I might die."

I know about people dying. Gramps died last year because he was very old. I went to his funeral. I was allowed to put Gramps's favourite seashell into his coffin.

"So if there's a chance of me not getting better and not being here anymore," I say, "then I want you to be a free tiger. A wild tiger, the sort of tiger you're *meant* to be."

"I'm *your* tiger," says Tiger. "And I don't like it when you say things like that."

"There's nothing to be scared of," I tell him. "You heard Frank. My raft won't sink for ages. You'll be able to jump off at a wild place, before it sinks. It'll be an adventure."

"What about this one?" says Frank. He hands me another twig.

"Perfect," I say. "That's all I need to finish. Can I sit by the water for a while now?"

"Sure thing. You want to launch your raft, right?"

"Right," I say.

I test the raft in the water. The creek pulls at it.

"It wants to take off," says Frank.

I take Tiger from my lap. I kiss him gently on his nose, and place him snugly inside the raft.

"Hey, are you sure you want to do that?" Frank asks.

"Yes," I say.

With his lopsided smile facing the adventure ahead, Tiger sets sail. The current catches the raft and carries it away, quickly.

"Goodbye, Tiger," I call out after him. "Good luck. I wish I was going with you."

"I'm ready to go back inside now," I say to Frank. "Please."

"Goodbye, Martin," Tiger calls out, as the raft spins him away. "I wish I didn't have to go."

Splashes of creek water wet Tiger's fur but the raft stays afloat. From far away Tiger can smell sea salt on the air, even though he doesn't really know what it is.

The raft gets caught in an eddy just where the creek splits in two, and it goes down the narrower branch, away from the sea.

It goes through tiger country on the outskirts of the big city.

And so, when the place is wild enough, Tiger leaps.

11

Henny Penny

Janice Leitch

Before Skippy went to live on a farm, she had no pets of her own.

"Wait until after we shift," her parents said. Now they had shifted, and Skippy was thinking about her pet.

Mum asked, "Did you see the kittens in the shed?"

"I don't want a kitten."

"How about a lamb?" asked Dad. "You'd have fun feeding a lamb, and you could enter it in the pet show."

Skippy thought about that. "Lambs grow to be big sheep. I don't want a lamb."

"Maybe a puppy?" asked Mum.

"How about a calf?" said Dad.

"You can't live in the country and not have a pet," said Mum.

Skippy looked at Dad. "How about that little brown chook in the hen house?"

"A chook!" said Dad. "The man who owned the farm

said all that chook is good for is chicken soup."

"Oh no, Dad! She's lovely. She lets me pick her up."

"Well, why not," said Dad. "But you'll have to look after all the hens, not just your little brown one."

"Thanks, Dad," said Skippy. She skipped out to the hen house. But the little brown hen wasn't worried about being anybody's pet that night. She was asleep on her perch, her head tucked under a wing.

"See you in the morning, Henny Penny," said Skippy.

Skippy and Henny Penny became best friends. They went everywhere together. Skippy would either carry Henny Penny tucked under her arm, or she'd put her into the doll's pram.

On pet show day, Skippy dressed Henny Penny in a doll's bonnet with the ribbon tied in a bow around her neck, and a cape that Mum had knitted for her. Then Skippy wheeled Henny Penny round in a pushchair decorated with crepe paper and big yellow sunflowers. They won the fancy dress first prize.

"If that hen would lay eggs she'd be the perfect pet," said Dad one day.

"She *is* the perfect pet," replied Skippy. "But she doesn't always want to come out with me. Sometimes she scratches around until she's made a nest, then gets cross if I move her."

"Henny Penny's clucky," said Mum. "She wants to sit on eggs and hatch out chickens."

"But she can't," wailed Skippy. "She hasn't laid any."

"Don't worry," said Dad, "I know someone who might be able to give us eggs for Henny Penny."

So that afternoon Dad built a nesting box for Henny Penny, then he drove off in the car for some eggs.

"He's back," Skippy called as the car came up the drive.

Dad was carrying a box with eight big eggs. Dad put the eggs in the nesting box, and Henny Penny popped in.

"When will they hatch?" Skippy kept asking.

"Not for a while," Dad said.

Time went slowly for Skippy, now that she couldn't take Henny Penny for walks any more. At last the great day arrived. The eggshells cracked, and the chickens began to hatch. Skippy could hardly believe her eyes. It wasn't eight chickens that popped out of the eggs, but eight fluffy little brown ducklings. "How can Henny Penny look after baby ducks?" wailed Skippy.

"That's strange," said Mum. "Dad didn't say anything about those being duck eggs. But we do need ducklings, Skippy. They'll be able to live on the pond by the willow tree."

"But she'll never be able to look after them," Skippy wailed again. "Poor Henny Penny!"

One morning the ducklings discovered there was water in the pond. Nothing could keep them out of there. Henny Penny ran round in circles, cackling and flapping her wings. Mum and Dad came to see what the noise was about.

"If only we had a boat," cried Skippy.

"I've got an idea," Dad ran back to the house.

"What's that he's carrying?" asked Mum when he came back.

"My lilo!" cried Skippy. She ran inside and put on her bathing suit.

Skippy held Henny Penny under her arm and sat on the lilo. Dad pushed, and they floated into the middle of the pond. The ducklings swam behind.

"Quack," said the ducklings.

"Here we are, Henny Penny," said Skippy.

"Cluck cluck," said the hen.

12

Dinosaurs at the Deluxe Dog Motel

Peter Friend

Steve was a world-famous movie director. Well, he hoped he would be, when he grew up. Right now, he was working on his first-ever film, called *Robot Warriors of Doom* unless he could think up a better title. He'd arranged twenty-seven toy robots on his bedroom floor, and was about to start the video camera when he heard odd noises from outside.

He looked out his upstairs bedroom window. He could see over the high wooden fence to next door where the noise came from — the Deluxe Dog Motel, one of those boarding kennel places where dogs stayed while their owners went away on holiday. It had gone out of business last year, and the building had been empty ever since.

But now a white truck was parked outside. Secretive-looking people carried in mysterious boxes marked 'Live — Handle With Care'.

Something clattered behind him. He turned and saw

that Fluffy the cat had knocked over his robots.

"Stupid cat!" he shouted, and chased her downstairs. She vanished out the cat door.

"Mum! Mad scientists are moving in next door!"

"That's nice, dear," said Mum, not even looking up.

"They're going to do evil experiments and breed rampaging monsters!"

"Really. And why are you chasing Fluffy?"

"She squashed my film set."

"Okay then, change your film to *Giant Killer Cat Versus the Robot Warriors of Doom*."

Hmmm. Mum didn't have good ideas very often, but Steve thought that this was a great idea. He went outside to look for Fluffy, but couldn't see her anywhere. He peered into the shrubbery where she liked to hide sometimes, by the dog motel fence.

Then he forgot all about Fluffy. Through the narrow gaps between the fence palings, he could see into one of the 'Live — Handle With Care' boxes.

A small dragon stared up at him. Steve stared back.

No, don't be silly, it couldn't be a dragon — no wings. It must be a baby dinosaur. Well, that proved those people must be mad scientists — they were genetically engineering dinosaurs.

He ran back to the house to tell Mum, but stopped at the door. She wouldn't believe him. He needed proof.

Of course — the video camera!

But when he returned with the camera, he noticed something strange. The dinosaur hadn't moved. Not at all, not even a millimetre.

He sighed. "You're not a real dinosaur at all, are you? Just a toy or a garden statue or something."

But then it did move, just a little. He pressed Record and waited for it to move again. Nothing happened for ages, then the dinosaur turned its head.

Oh. From this angle, it looked familiar somehow. Steve rummaged in his jeans and found a five-cent coin. Yup. The creature was a tuatara, just like the one on the coin.

He ran inside. "Mum! The mad scientists are doing evil experiments on tuataras!" He pressed Play on the video camera and showed her the screen.

"It does look like a tuatara," she admitted, and went out to see for herself. She soon returned, frowning. "Something funny's going on. Tuataras are a protected species — what are they doing around here? I'm going to ring the Department of Conservation."

She did. Someone transferred her to someone else and then someone else, and eventually she had to explain everything four times and sounded rather annoyed. "Yes, we're at the end of Chamberlain Road, just like I told the other three people. What? Yes, this is a cordless phone. Go outside? What for?"

She went out to the back yard, followed by Steve.

"Hi," said a voice. They looked up over the fence, and there was one of the mad scientists, holding a cellphone and grinning. "I'm Neville; I work for the Department of Conservation. You'd better pop around."

So they went next door. The building looked the same as ever, with the peeling 'Deluxe Dog Motel' sign still on the front wall.

The door squeaked open and Neville waved them inside. "Apparently us scientists aren't too good at designing top-secret hideaways," he said.

"I told you they were mad scientists," Steve reminded Mum.

Neville laughed. "Only a bit mad. We're a tuatara breeding programme. We had a fire at our headquarters last week, and this is our temporary location while repairs are done. I'd hoped no one would notice us. We'll only be here a few weeks, but I'd appreciate it if you'd keep us a secret. There are wildlife smugglers who'd love to get their slimy hands on a few tuataras — worth a fortune overseas. Judy's installing our alarm system now." He pointed at a woman on a ladder, who was busy connecting cables.

Steve and Mum promised they wouldn't tell anyone. Neville showed them around the dog motel's sunny back yard, where dozens of glass-sided boxes were now occupied by sunbathing tuataras.

"Are they all this lazy?" Steve asked. "I'm making a movie, and now I'm thinking of calling it *Giant Killer Dinosaur Versus the Robot Warriors of Doom*. I was wondering if maybe I could borrow a tuatara. Please?"

"Sounds exciting," said Neville. "But a tuatara would be a terrible movie star. Some days the only times they move is to crawl into the sun in the morning and then back into their burrows at night. And by the way, they're not actual dinosaurs, although they were around at the same time as the dinosaurs. I've got a life-sized plastic tuatara here somewhere — you can use that for your movie if you like."

He rummaged through cluttered cardboard boxes and

eventually found a cool tuatara model as long as Steve's arm.

"Thanks," said Steve. "I'll take really good care of it."

He renamed his movie *Giant Killer Tuatara Versus the Robot Warriors of Doom Versus the Giant Killer Cat*. Fluffy turned out to be quite a good actor, so long as Steve smeared cat food on the robots first.

Filming took up all the next week, and he still hadn't finished by bedtime on Sunday night. Yawning, he pushed the robots under his bed and went to the window to pull the curtains.

Strange. It was almost dark outside, but he could see a white truck parked outside the Deluxe Dog Motel, and people moving around. Was it Neville's truck? He took the video camera over to the window and pressed the Night-View Button. Everything onscreen looked green and fuzzy, but he could see enough — someone was climbing over the fence.

"Mum, wildlife smugglers are breaking in next door!"

"Are you sure?" asked Mum. "I don't —"

A squealing alarm siren interrupted her. She and Steve ran outside, only to see the truck speeding away.

Neville arrived ten minutes later, looking very annoyed. "We've got a good idea who's behind this, but the police can't do anything without some evidence," he said.

"I recorded them on videotape in Night-View mode," said Steve. "You can't see the people that well, but the truck's number plate shows up great."

Neville grinned. "Good thinking, Steve. With instincts like that, you'll be a great movie director one day."

"So he keeps telling everyone," said Mum.

Wool You Join Us?

David Hill

When I came into Room Ten on Wednesday morning, all the kids were down the far end.

The girls were going, "Oh, so cute!"

The guys were going, "Looks like you, Jarrod . . . Nah, looks like you, Matiu."

I pushed through the crowd of kids, and stared. It was a poodle. No, a baby goat. No, a — "It's a lamb!" I said.

"Hey," went Matiu. "What do you call stories told by a baby sheep? Lamb's Tales."

Tamsin had brought the lamb to school. "She's our first lamb born this year," Tamsin said. "Her mother had twins, but she hasn't got enough milk for both of them, so we're feeding this one from a bottle."

"Hey," went Matiu. "What do you get when you cross a lamb with a kangaroo? A woolly jumper."

Tamsin took no notice of him. She pulled a baby's bottle out of her bag, and next minute — Glomp! The lamb was

72

sucking away flat out. Her head bunted, her tail waggled, milk dribbled down her chin. Just like my little sister Stacey — except for the tail.

"What's she called, Tamsin?" our teacher Ms Mika asked.

"Yeah," said Jarrod. "Is she called Baaaarbie?"

"No," Tamsin told him. "She's called Pam. Pam the Lamb."

Pam the Lamb curled up on the floor beside Tamsin's desk. A couple of times she went "Baaaa!" So all Room Ten went "Baaaa!" back to her — until Ms Mika said that anyone who kept doing that would end up on a baaaarbecue.

Pam had another bottle at interval. "Why's she shaking?" someone asked. "All lambs shake," said Andrew, who lives on a farm like Tamsin. "It's because their hearts beat so fast."

"Hey," went Matiu. "What did the farmer say to insult the lady sheep? Ewe Idiot!"

After interval, we had Personal Writing. "I'm going to write some nursery rhymes," Ripeka Matthews announced. "Tamsin had a little lamb . . . "

"Yeah," said Jarrod. "Tamsin had a little lamb. A little pork. A little ham . . ."

We'd been writing for about ten minutes when Tamsin looked down at Pam and put her hand up. "Er . . . Ms Mika? Pam's done a puddle on the floor."

She *is* like my little sister Stacey, I thought. Ms Mika sighed. "Find Mr Chan the caretaker. Get some disinfectant and a bucket of water."

At lunchtime, Tamsin put a leash on Pam's collar and

73

we took her outside. The guys all wanted to teach Pam how to play soccer, but Tamsin said no, she and her friends were going to read Pam some Hairy Maclary stories.

"Hairy Maclary?" Jarrod asked. "Don't you mean Woolly MacPully?"

"Hey," went Matiu. "What did the sailor call when he saw the lamb's parents? Sheep Ahoy!"

After lunch, we had our usual Wednesday Afternoon Girls versus Guys Word-Quiz. The girls said that Pam was going to be in their team.

"Now," said Ms Mika. "What's the name for a bank of sand formed when a river meets the sea? A sand . . . ?"

"Baaaa!" went Pam.

"Right!" said Ms Mika. "A sand bar. Well done, Pam. A point for the girls."

"Awww!" groaned all the guys.

"Next word," said Ms Mika. "The name for the part of a bike you steer with. A handle . . . ?"

"Baaaa!" went Pam again.

"Right!" said Ms Mika. "Another point for the girls."

"Awww!" groaned all the guys again.

When the quiz was over, Pam had some more milk, and went to sleep beside Tamsin's desk.

After a while Jarrod suddenly yelled, "Look! Pam's eating my science project!"

She was, too. A piece of green paper was just vanishing into her mouth. "What's your project about, Jarrod?" someone asked.

"It's about healthy diets," Jarrod replied. "Why's everyone laughing?"

"Hey," went Matiu. "What did the man sing when he was shearing the friendly sheep? 'Fleece A Jolly Good Fellow'."

We worked on for another quarter of an hour. Then Tamsin looked down and put up her hand again. "Er . . . Ms Mika?"

"Another puddle?" our teacher asked.

"Ummm . . . not a *puddle* exactly," Tamsin said. Sure enough, kids near her desk were holding their noses.

Ms Mika sighed again. "Find Mr Chan the caretaker. Get some disinfectant and a *big* bucket of water."

When we were packing up that afternoon, Ms Mika said, "Andrew, if any lambs are born on *your* farm tonight, just bring a photo of them." Andrew grinned.

Next morning in class, Ms Mika was calling out everyone's names. Andrew wasn't there. Then the door opened, and Andrew looked in. He was holding a rope tied to something outside. "Hey, Ms Mika . . ." he began.

Our teacher stared. "Andrew, I told you not to bring any lambs along!"

Andrew shook his head. "Nah. Nah, I haven't brought a lamb."

"MOOOOO!" went the something outside.

14

Charley Two

Lorraine Orman

Patrick had just arrived for his summer holiday with his grandparents at Omaha Beach. As usual he ran into the lounge to talk to Charley, their cheeky white cockatiel. But the cage wasn't there in its usual corner. "Where's Charley?" he demanded.

"Oh dear, I knew we should have told him when it happened," Gran said.

"Patrick, Charley died a month ago," Grandad said. "He was very old. It was time for him to go."

"He's dead?" asked Patrick disbelievingly.

"I'm afraid so," replied Grandad.

"I don't want him to be dead!" Patrick cried. "He wasn't old! It's not fair!"

Gran tried to give him a cuddle, but Patrick felt all mixed up inside: sad and angry at the same time. Who was he going to talk to when Gran and Grandad were busy? Who was going to nibble his earlobes and pull his hair and screech, "Awk! Who's a pretty boy then? Charley wants a biscuit!"

Patrick rushed outside with his skateboard and skated along the footpaths in the new housing subdivision next to his grandparents' house. There were no buildings yet. It was just sand and shells and stones and spiky sea-grass. His skateboard made a rough, angry noise on the concrete.

Suddenly Patrick noticed a bird moving on the sand a few metres away. It was slightly smaller than a seagull. It had dappled brown wings, a white body with a pink chest, and a long black beak. It was scrabbling crookedly over the sand, dragging one wing behind it. It kept on cheeping loudly and cocking its head to look back at him.

"Hey," said Patrick, "Have you hurt your wing?" He started walking slowly towards the bird. He didn't want to frighten it. The bird hopped for another few metres, watching him all the time. Suddenly it spread its wings and flew gracefully into the air. There was nothing wrong with its wing. Weird, thought Patrick.

When Patrick told Grandad about the bird, Grandad laughed. "That was a New Zealand dotterel," he said. "Tuturiwhatu. She was luring you away from her nest by pretending to be hurt."

"There's a nest somewhere there?" Patrick said. "Choice! I'm going to find it!"

Grandad shook his head. "The dotterels are endangered," he said. "There are only about fifteen hundred of them left in the whole world.

We have to look after them very carefully. That dotterel was foolish to lay her eggs in the middle of the subdivision. She should have laid them in the protected areas on the sand-spit, where people aren't allowed to walk."

Patrick thought about this. "Then I'll find the nest and make sure it stays safe," he said.

"What a good idea," said Grandad.

When the dotterel did her wing-dragging trick again, Patrick stood on the footpath and looked carefully at the sandy area behind her. After a very long time he spotted a small, speckled egg. It was sitting in a slight hollow in the sand. "What a silly bird!" he said to the dotterel. "That's a useless place to lay an egg."

Grandad helped Patrick build a fence along the section of footpath closest to the nest. They stuck garden stakes into the sand, with lengths of green plastic tape tied between them. Patrick attached a piece of cardboard to the fence that said, "Beware — dotterel nest."

Every morning he skated into the subdivision and sat down on the footpath for half an hour and watched the dotterel. After a few days she got used to him being there,

and she didn't even stand up when he arrived. She just watched him with her big, dark eyes. Patrick decided that if birds could smile, she was smiling at him.

Patrick did a lot of thinking while he minded the dotterel. He thought of all the clever things Charley could say. He remembered how Charley was always so pleased to see him, chattering and screeching with delight. And how Charley used to clamber nimbly round the cage, swinging by his beak and his claws. Patrick laughed as he remembered. Then he thought about the fact that there were only fifteen hundred New Zealand dotterels left in the whole world. That certainly wasn't something to laugh about.

On the days when it rained, Patrick borrowed Grandad's oilskin jacket and sat on the footpath with the jacket over his head like a yellow tent. When he peered out, he was sure the dotterel was chuckling at him. "It's your fault if I look stupid," he said to her.

Once he'd done his daily stint of bird-sitting, Patrick was ready to go down to the beach with Gran and Grandad and enjoy the rest of the day, swimming and boogie-boarding and playing cricket on the sand.

Then came a day when the dotterel wasn't there. Patrick crawled under the fence and crept closer to the nest site. He couldn't see the egg either. There was the little hollow — but no egg. Patrick stared all around, his heart thumping. What had happened to it? Had a seagull eaten it? Or a stoat? Maybe some stupid person had come along and trodden on it. Grandad had told him about the bad things that could happen to an unprotected egg lying on the sand.

Patrick felt like crying. He kept on looking around. Maybe it had got shifted somehow. Maybe the mother dotterel had moved it to a safer place. *Where was it?*

Then his eye caught a tiny movement underneath a bush. He peered hard. Suddenly his eyes seemed to focus properly, and he realised he was looking at a chick crouched there: a fluffy, speckly, little chick. It was sitting as still as a stone. Grandad had said that dotterel chicks were very good at being invisible while their parents were away gathering food. But Patrick could see its tiny black eye, and he knew the chick was looking back at him.

Patrick's throat choked up again. But this time it was with joy, not with sadness. "Hello, Number 1501," he called. "Welcome to the world. But I don't want to call you that. I'm going to call you Charley Two. Hello, Charley Two."

The chick turned its head slightly so it could watch him better. It opened its beak as if it was about to cheep. Perhaps it was saying hello.

"Who's a pretty boy then?" Patrick sang, just the way Charley used to say it.

And he raced home on his skateboard, thrumming over the concrete, to tell Grandad the excellent news.

15

Bone Growing

Janice Marriott

Dog and Cat were in the garden, watching their pet human planting seeds. Cat was bored — so bored that she started talking to Dog. "What are you eating?"

Dog replied, "A teeny weeny bone. It's all I've got. Our pet human is too busy gardening to feed me properly."

They both stretched and turned in the sun, to get a better look at their mysterious pet human.

Cat complained, "All that working he's doing is making me tired."

Dog agreed. "It wouldn't be so bad if he was doing something useful. What *is* he doing, do you think?"

"He's burying teeny weeny seeds in the soil and then he's patting the soil and stroking it," said Cat, staring hard at their pet human.

Dog dropped his bone. "Now, why would he want to do that?"

Cat washed herself with long lazy strokes. "You don't

understand much, do you?" she said.

Dog looked sad. "I understand how to crunch bones, and how to sniff for other dogs' pee mails and —"

"You don't understand gardening," announced Cat. "See. Those teeny weeny seeds are hard and dry —"

"Just like my bone!" interrupted Dog, wagging his tail.

Cat continued. "He buries them to soften them and —"
"I do that! I do that!" barked Dog.

"They grow and —"

Dog howled, "They *grow*! Really! That's amazing!"

Cat looked down her nose at Dog who was rolling on the grass and waggling his legs in the air.

"Yes," she continued. "When the seeds get wet from the rain in the soil, they grow bigger and bigger until —"

"Wooof! Until what? What?" Dog was jumping up and down. Thrashing his tail from side to side.

"I'm not telling you any more if you keep interrupting me," said Cat, settling into tight ball shape, with her tail wrapped over her head. Dog pawed the ground.

"Go on!" he barked.

Cat pretended to be reluctant. In fact she loved the sound of her own voice, and she loved getting Dog over-excited.

"Until they become huge," she said softly.

"Huge? What?" woofed Dog. "Hu-ooo-ge? You mean the bones? Wow!" He chased his tail because he couldn't stay still. "Huge, huge bones! No! That would be a dream come true!"

Cat smirked. "Yes," she purred. "Some of the seeds get huge under the ground, like potatoes. And some get big and juicy above ground, like tomatoes. And then —" She stopped to clean her tail, very slowly.

"What? Quick, tell me!" yapped Dog, dribbling now.

Cat lowered her leg, pointing her foot. "The human digs them up and eats them."

Cat and Dog stared at each other.

"Amazing!" wuffed Dog. "Totally miraculous!"

Dog raced round and round the garden. He couldn't stop himself. The pet human straightened up and looked at him.

"You're a mad dog, you are. I'm just going out to get some compost for the seeds. I won't be long." He put down his spade and picked up his jacket, then he left them.

Dog and Cat lay in the shade but Dog couldn't keep still. He was thinking. Very soon he had a cunning plan.

He said to Cat, as casually as possible, "I'll just bury this teeny weeny bone." He got up, stretched, picked up the bone and trotted down the garden path. He looked around quickly to check Cat was not watching. He didn't want Cat seeing his thoughts.

Very carefully and thoroughly, Dog dug a huge hole in the soil where the seeds were planted. He gently planted his teeny weeny bone at the bottom of the hole. Now I'll pat the soil and stroke it, he thought. He raked the soil back over the bone with his big paws. Soil was flung everywhere. And I'll just water it a tiny bit, he thought. He stood, with his eyes closed, on three legs, while he watered the bone.

He waggled back up the path to where Cat was lying in the sun with her eyes shut. He stretched out beside her, his eyes wide open. "I'll just lie here quietly and watch that huge hill I've made," he said.

They both pretended to sleep. After twenty seconds, Dog leaped up. "Do you think my bone's growing yet, Cat?"

"No! It takes weeks, sometimes months. You have to be patient."

Dog howled. Then he ran round the garden once more. I can be patient. I can be patient, he panted. I'll have a sleep.

Much later, their pet human returned. He opened the garden gate and smiled at the two sleeping animals.

"Hello, pets. How are you lovely — WHAT IS THAT HUGE HILL IN THE GARDEN? WHAT HAS BEEN GOING ON?" Human roared with anger.

Dog looked confused, his head on one side. Cat slunk away into the shade. The pet human grabbed the spade and dug into the hill Dog had made in his vegetable garden. He dug and dug until he pulled out the teeny weeny bone.

Dog whimpered.

"Dog!" yelled Human, "I am very cross with you. I

bought you a big bone at the shop but I won't give it to you now. You don't deserve it."

Human picked up the grocery bag and disappeared into his huge house. Dog crawled into his tiny kennel. He was totally miserable. Then his nose whiffled. He smelt his teeny weeny bone. It was lying where the pet human had thrown it. Dog trotted out to collect it.

On the way back he passed Cat, stretched out on the garden seat, pretending to be asleep. "Humans are just so impatient," whined Dog. "No wonder they have to buy bones at the shop instead of growing their own."

16

Don't Feed the Keas

Darlene Thomson

Something was different. I knew it the second I woke up. The constant drip drip drip of water into the ice-cream container beside my stretcher had stopped. I jumped out of my sleeping bag, leapt over the sleeping bodies and unzipped the tent flaps. Yes! The rain had stopped.

"Dad, Dad, wake up!" I shouted into his sleepy face. "Today's the day. Hurry, get up!"

"It's only six o'clock, Chrissie," he moaned, looking at his watch. But when he saw I wasn't going to leave him alone, he crawled out of his bag.

All Christmas holidays he'd promised we'd climb Rob Roy Glacier so I could see some keas. The trouble was, it had rained non-stop for the last week and there were only two more days left of our holiday. If we didn't go today, I knew we never would.

Dad and my big brother had always gone tramping into the mountains so they'd seen lots of keas, but until this year they'd said I was too little so I still hadn't seen a *real live* one. I knew lots of things about keas, like how they're really curious and will eat anything and everything — it doesn't even have to be food.

Dad once told me about this car that was parked up on a ski field. It was old fashioned with a soft vinyl roof. Some keas landed on it and had a picnic. They pecked it to bits. When they'd finished it looked like a convertible with its top down. They'd even chewed the rubber from around the windows. When the owner opened his door, the window fell out and the windscreen fell in. Dad said it was pretty funny, but it just goes to show how naughty keas are.

Dad nudged Jake to wake him, but he rolled over and mumbled something not very nice under his breath, so we left him there. Within minutes I had Dad organized and we were on our way. During the drive I kept asking him questions.

"Tell me again — how big are keas? Tell me again — where do they sleep? Tell me again — what sound do they make?" After each answer Dad gave me he always added, "If you forget everything else, you mustn't forget the number one rule: DON'T FEED THE KEAS! Nothing but trouble ever comes from feeding keas."

When we got to the car park in a big paddock, Dad put the car keys into his pocket. "We don't want to lose those way up there or we'll have real problems," he said, pointing to the top of the glacier, just visible under the clouds.

Every few minutes during our long climb, Dad asked very seriously, "What is it you have to remember, Chrissie?"

"DON'T FEED THE KEAS," I'd reply and Dad gave me

the thumbs-up. I couldn't wait till we reached the top.

To my disappointment, there wasn't a single kea anywhere. There were signs telling us all about them, but no real live ones. Dad said to be patient. It's hard to be patient when you've been waiting your whole life to see something.

We sat down facing the blue glacier and began eating our muesli bars. The shiny paper glistened in the sun, and curious, hungry keas surrounded us at once. They were even more beautiful than I'd imagined. Their bright colours were so vivid compared to the white snow and the grey rocks. They hopped around me, getting closer and closer all the time. It was wonderful.

"Don't feed them," Dad warned me for the millionth time. I put the rest of my muesli bar in my jacket pocket and zipped it up. When a kea was close enough for me to touch, Dad quietly reached into his pack for the camera.

As he did so, the car keys slipped out of his pocket and onto the ground. The sun shone — the keys glittered — and a kea snuck behind Dad, snatched them up and flew away.

We chased it over sharp rocks, into a freezing stream  and through some cutty grass yelling, "Give us back our keys!" Finally the kea landed on a sheer rock-face that was completely unclimbable. It waved the keys back and forth in its beak — they made a mocking tune as they struck one another. The kea was teasing us, letting us know that this was its home and up here it was smarter than we were.

Running his hands through his hair, Dad sighed. "Now what're we going to do? We're hours from camp and a cell-phone won't work here."

I caught sight of some keas in the distance, pecking in the snow for food, and had an idea. I pulled out a chocolate bar that I'd been saving for our tramp down. Noisily I tore open the wrapper and flashed the silver paper in the sun. As if by magic the thieving kea reappeared, with our car keys still dangling from its beak.

I hoped it would only be able to hold either the chocolate or the keys, not both. So I laid the treat down on the ground, at my feet. Sure enough the kea dropped the keys, grabbed the chocolate and flew away. I stepped on the keys before another kea decided it wanted to play games with us too.

As I handed the keys back to Dad, I told him, "Sometimes, Dad, you *have* to feed the keas."

17

The Weta in the Letterbox

Wanda Cowley

"Nobody loves me," said Weta.

"What about your mother?" asked Spider.

"She went away," said Weta. "And she didn't come back." He crawled further into the corner of the letterbox to get away from the light.

"Come on," said Spider. "What about Girl? She says you are her knight in shining armour."

"She keeps going away."

"But she sends letters with messages for you on the envelopes, at least one a week. And she keeps coming back."

"Not this last time," said Weta.

"What about Gran? She says she knows her letters will be safe as long as you live in her box."

"But she's gone away too."

"She'll come back," said Spider. "She always comes back."

"Not this last time," said Weta. "Didn't you hear all those sirens wailing and everyone talking at once? The ambulance took her away to hospital."

"But Postie comes every day. She calls, 'Yoo-hoo, Weta, Here's a letter.' She doesn't call out to me."

Weta sighed. "When Gran was here she would open the door and say, 'Gidday, Weta. Can I have my letter?' Then she would say 'Have a good sleep', and close the door. Now Mrs Next Door comes clip-clip-clippety-clip along the path take the letters out. Yesterday, when she saw me, she shrieked, 'EEEEEEEEEK! Help! Someone come and kill the weta!'"

"Good thing you got away before Help arrived with her broom," said Spider.

"That's all past now. I know when to hide." Weta waved his feelers. "But I think there's more trouble coming. What about all these ants rushing around the floor? I think they're going to build a nest."

"Ssh!" said Spider. "I hear Postie."

They listened to the rumble of Postie's motorbike as it stopped and started, stopped and started, getting nearer and nearer. Then it stopped by the letterbox. "Yoo-hoo, Weta. Here's two letters."

It wasn't long before Mrs Next Door clip, clip clippety clipped along the path.

Weta and Spider hid in the ceiling corners and watched the door open to reveal a cross face.

"Oh No!" moaned Mrs Next Door "The letters are covered with ants." She shut the door with a bang. "Kill! Spray! Exterminate!" she yelled.

"Off you go, Weta," said Spider. "I'm off too. We'll have to stay away until the air has cleared."

Weta crawled out the letter opening and into the hedge while Spider tried to get the ants to follow. But they were too busy to listen, so Spider went to join Weta.

They watched Mrs Next Door come and spray the inside of the letterbox. In the afternoon she came back and swept up the dead ants. She left the door open and went away.

"Let's go back inside," said Weta.

"No," said Spider. "It won't be safe until tomorrow."

So they stayed in the hedge until the sun set. Then it was time for Weta to go and find some dinner and for Spider to build a web.

In the morning they stayed in the hedge until Mrs Next Door came and closed the door of the letterbox. Then they climbed back inside.

"Time for your sleep," said Spider.

Weta yawned. "I'll just wait to see if there's a message for me."

It seemed a long time before they heard the rumble of

Postie's bike. "Yoo-hoo, Weta," she called. "Here's some letters."

Weta stretched his legs, waggled his feelers and crawled over to the letters to see if there was a message for him.

"Who's it from?" asked Spider. "What does it say?"

"It's from Girl. She says 'See you soon.'"

"Shush," said Spider. "That sounds like Gran's car."

They listened as the car turned into the drive and stopped by the letterbox.

"I'll get the letters, Gran," called Girl.

The door opened. "Hello, my knight in shining armour," said Girl as she picked up the letters. "I'll shut out the light and let you get back to sleep."

"She didn't say hello to me," said Spider. "Nobody loves me."

"I do," said Weta.

18

Bonecrusher

Janice Leitch

I didn't realise Melanie was interested in eels until the day an apple core bounced off my head. Melanie was up a tree, reading.

"Listen to this," she said. "You can only catch eels when there's an 'R' in the month!"

I thought about that for a moment, then said: "There's an R in November, and that's this month. Hey, let's go eeling!"

The best person to talk to about eeling is our Uncle Barney. We jumped on our bikes and raced out to the farm. Aunty Tui was about to pour Uncle Barney's cup of tea. He likes his tea really strong. "No good if you can't stand a spoon up in it," he says. Aunty Tui uses five tea bags. It's not really a waste though, because when she's poured Uncle Barney's brew, the teabags can be used for us. We like our tea to be on the weak side. We hate to spoil the taste of Aunty Tui's pikelets and raspberry jam.

Once we'd finished afternoon tea, Melanie settled down to business. "Ever been eeling, Uncle Barney?"

"Eeling?" said Uncle Barney. "Have I been eeling! Used to be the best eeler around! Speared 'em, and netted 'em. Almost caught old Bonecrusher once. Now he really was an eel — a monster!"

"A monster!" said Melanie. "How big? Is he still there? Could we catch him?"

"Haven't heard tell of old Bonecrusher for a while," said Uncle Barney. "He'd be old — about twenty, and he'd be pretty big — at least four metres, and as thick as a tree. Ferocious too. He's been known to steal lambs."

"Wow," said Melanie. "Now that's what I'd call a real eel. I'd love to hook him. Could we go eeling, Uncle Barney? Would you take us?"

Uncle Barney scratched his head. "Dunno about that," he said. "Gave my spear away years ago. And my net's rotted."

But Melanie was ready for anything. "That's all right," she said. "I'll make us hand lines, real strong ones. Would they do?"

"Hand lines!" laughed Uncle Barney. "Hand lines? Yes, I suppose they'd work. Okay, Melanie, we'll go eeling sometime."

"How about tonight?" I asked. "The forecast is fine weather." I had my fingers crossed behind my back, wishing he'd say yes.

Aunty Tui interrupted. "What about a barbecue down at the river? If we took some sausages and some eggs, we could have a night out."

At six o'clock we piled into Uncle Barney's truck and took off for the river. When I asked Uncle Barney how old his truck was, he said he'd had it for sixty years. I know the truck's old, but I think he was exaggerating.

It's great riding in Uncle Barney's truck, bumping across the paddocks. The truck hasn't any springs, so you bounce up and down. We had an argument over who would be the best eeler.

"You catch as many as you like," said Melanie. "I'm going to get the biggest eel ever!"

We found a good spot by a clump of willows, near a bend in the river. Uncle Barney thought it was the same place where he fished years ago.

Melanie baited up the hooks with Uncle Barney's best dog tucker, and started fishing. Aunty Tui spread her rug on a grassy bank where she could watch how the eeling progressed. When I saw Uncle Barney putting out the barbecue I rushed over to help. I caught my foot in a hole. I bumped into Uncle Barney, sending the pile of bread he held spinning into the river. There was a swirling and splashing where the bread hit. In seconds the bread was gone; only a few ripples ruffled the surface.

"What was that?" I gasped.

"Was that a fish?" asked Aunty Tui.

"They must sure be hungry tonight!" said Uncle Barney.

"Hey, you're not meant to be feeding them!" Melanie shouted.

We all started the serious business of fishing. I was first to get a bite, much to Melanie's disgust. My line had only been down for about two minutes when something tugged. I stood up and jerked the line as hard as I could.

"That's the way," said Uncle Barney. "Make sure he's well hooked. Now pull him in. Slowly, slowly, that's the way."

I pulled at my line, keeping it taut so there was no slack that could let my eel wriggle off. I pulled and pulled. My arms were really aching. Melanie came over for a look as I dragged it up the bank.

Uncle Barney took my eel off the hook, put it in a sack he'd brought with him, and winked. "Not big," he said. "But it will be nice smoked."

Uncle Barney caught one next. I got two more, I managed to land them and get the hooks out by myself.

We'd been fishing for an hour, but still Melanie hadn't had a bite. I think part of that was her fault; she would keep on hauling in her line to make sure the bait was still there.

"Leave it in the water," said Uncle Barney after she'd pulled up her line for the millionth time. "You'll know when an eel's hooked!"

Then Melanie squealed. "I've got something," she yelled. "It's huge, I can't pull it in!" She tried hard, but after only a minute the eel broke free. It escaped with the bait, hooks and sinker. Melanie slid down the bank and almost followed the eel into the water.

"Have another go," said Uncle Barney. "There are plenty of spare hooks."

That eel must have taken a fancy to Melanie's bait. Again and again it snapped off everything.

Aunty Tui stood beside the water with her camera. The flash was ready for a photo of Melanie's monster. Then we saw its tail thrashing around on the surface. When she saw how big it was, Aunty Tui decided to stay well out of the way and climbed up the bank.

"Think you've got old Bonecrusher there!" shouted Uncle Barney when Melanie hauled a bare line in for the fifth time. "Crikey, it's years since I last saw him!"

The next time Melanie hooked Bonecrusher, she passed her line to Uncle Barney. "My arms are sore," she said. "You have a go."

Uncle Barney heaved and pulled, heaved and pulled, and slowly drew the eel closer to the shore. Finally, he dragged the eel up onto the bank, where Bonecrusher twisted himself round and round the fishing line — then Melanie's line broke — the giant eel was free.

But Bonecrusher didn't go straight back into the river. Oh no! Do you know what that cheeky eel did? He slithered over to our barbecue, snapped the sausages and bacon off the plate, and gulped them down. Then he slithered back into the water.

"Old Bonecrusher sure knows a thing or two about fishing!" said Uncle Barney. "I think we were the ones caught this time!"

19

Mad About Elephants

Margaret Beames

Two days before the school trip Andrew found some itchy red spots on his chest. By bedtime there were more — lots more — and he wasn't feeling too good.

"Chickenpox," said the doctor.

"Oh dear," said Mum. "He'll miss the school trip."

Miss the trip! "But I can't. We're going to the zoo!" Andrew cried. "They've got elephants there!"

"We'll take you when you're better," Mum said. "He's mad about elephants," she explained to the doctor.

Andrew couldn't believe he was going to miss the visit to the zoo, all because of rotten chickenpox. He'd been looking forward to the trip for ages.

"We'll go later," said Dad, but Andrew didn't want to go later. He wanted to go with his friends from school and he wanted to go NOW.

Mum brought him a jigsaw of elephants, bright with all the colours of India. "It's too hard. There are too many pieces," Andrew grumbled.

Dad found a book called *Babar the Elephant*, it was pretty good, too, and it was nice having Dad read to him but, "I want to see a *real* elephant!" Andrew whined.

Gran sent him a stuffed elephant made of blue velvet. Andrew threw it across the room. "I'm not a baby!" he yelled.

"You're acting like one," said his mother. "What would you like for tea?"

"An elephant!" he shouted. "A real one!"

"I'll boil you an egg," said Mum.

Andrew felt hot. His head ached and his spots itched. Mum dabbed them with special pink stuff. She gave him a fresh, cool pillow and before long he was asleep.

Much later, Andrew woke with a start. It felt like the middle of the night. The house was very quiet and his room was dark, just a faint light from the passage shining through his open bedroom door, but something had woken him. He sat up.

There was something different about the light. It was greenish, as if it was shining through leaves. Like a jungle, he thought. A long arm — no, a trunk — waved through the doorway, followed by a heavy head with tusks. Wow! An elephant!

It was not a very large elephant at first, although even as he watched it seemed to grow, so that it squeezed against the door frame. Once it was in, it seemed to fill his room. It bumped against the table, making everything on it rattle.

"Hey! You're real!" Andrew gasped. "How did you get here?"

"You called me," said the elephant. "I distinctly heard you. 'An elephant,' you shouted. 'A real one.'"

"Neat," said Andrew.

The elephant swung its big head from side to side, looking around the room. Its small bright eyes under their long eyelashes spotted an apple by Andrew's bed and with one smooth sweep of its trunk it scooped it into its mouth. "Have you got any more of those?" the elephant asked.

"In the kitchen," said Andrew. He ran along the passage to the kitchen and brought all the apples in the fridge. The elephant ate them. It burped and said, "Pardon me."

Andrew could hear a deep rumbling coming from its stomach. "Are you still hungry?" he asked.

"Of course I am. You need a lot of food when you're as big as me."

Andrew ran back to the kitchen. What was there that an elephant would like? He found a bag of carrots, a cabbage, some celery, a lettuce and some tomatoes. With his arms full, he struggled back to his bedroom.

The elephant ate everything except the lettuce. That he dropped and stepped on. "Hey, don't do that!" Andrew cried, looking at the squashy green mess on the carpet.

"I'm thirsty," said the elephant.

Andrew fetched a bucket of water from the laundry. It was very heavy and much of it slopped on to the floor and soaked his feet. The elephant emptied the bucket with one long slurp of its trunk.

"Any chance of a bath?" it asked.

"No!" cried Andrew, imagining the mess bathing an elephant would make in his room.

"Never mind," said the elephant. "Scratch my back instead."

So Andrew fetched a stiff brush from the laundry and scrubbed away at the elephant's wrinkled grey hide. "Harder," said the elephant. "That's better, behind my ears, that's it. Perfect."

Andrew's arms were aching. His feet were wet. He was tired. He'd really like to go back to bed, he thought. "Wouldn't you like to go to sleep now?" he asked hopefully. Did elephants sleep standing up, like horses?

"No, I have to go out," said the elephant.

Andrew looked at the size of it. He looked at the door. "You can't," he said.

"I HAVE TO GO OUT," the elephant repeated. It headed for the door.

"YOU CAN'T!" Andrew cried. Oh dear, this was awful. How was he going to explain where all that stuff from the fridge had gone? And the squashed lettuce? The water on the floor? Now it looked as if the door was about to be broken down. Either that, or there was going to be some-thing really disgusting on the carpet!

"Go away!" he cried. "You're too big. I'm tired and I want to go to sleep." He flung himself into bed and pulled the covers over his head. He listened but there was no sound from the elephant. Was it still there, waiting for him?

After a while he must have gone to sleep, for the next thing he knew Mum was there, opening the curtains. "Feeling better?" she asked. "Dad says if it's fine on Sunday we can all go to the zoo then and see those elephants you're so mad about."

Andrew was silent. "Er, Mum," he said at last, "how about we go to the Science Museum instead?"

"Good idea," said Mum. "They've got a great exhibition on, all about elephants and mammoths. You'll enjoy that. Andrew? What's the matter? Why are you hiding under the quilt? What do you mean — *no more elephants?*"

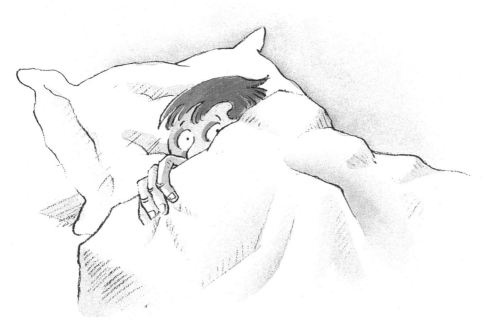

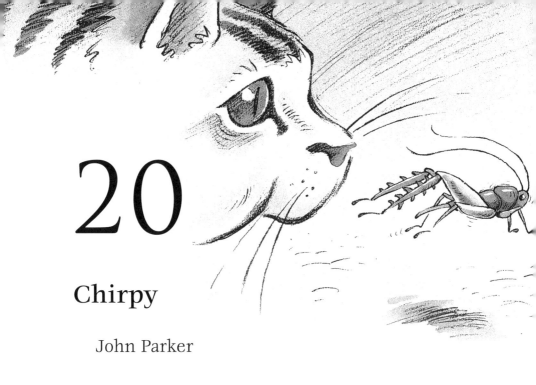

20

Chirpy

John Parker

It was dark when Smoky padded into the kitchen from outside, meowing in the muffled way that said her jaws were clamped around something.

Kevin saw spiky black legs dangling from the cat's mouth. It was a cricket. When the cat dropped it on the cork tiles, it stayed still.

Usually they hopped and jumped — but only on the same spot. Smoky always seemed to know how to cripple them so she could prod and play with them before she ended the one-sided game with a scrunch.

You've overdone it this time, old Smoky, thought Kevin. This one's dead meat. He pushed the cat away and bent down to pick up the cricket — but it came to life, wriggling in his cupped hands.

Kevin got a shock. It slipped through his fingers onto the floor. Smoky pounced. The cricket dodged her paws by a millimetre, scuttled along the toe-line of the sink

104

cupboards and disappeared underneath the dishwasher.

After a few minutes Smoky lost interest, wandering into the lounge to be with Kevin's father, who was watching TV. Kevin shone a torch underneath the dishwasher and round the sides. The beam showed cobwebs, dust and a couple of old salted peanuts — but not the cricket. As good as gone, Kevin thought. It's probably injured and will end up dying in there.

Then it gave a faint hesitant chirp — as if it was trying out its voice, surprised it was still alive. Then a second chirp, clearer and stronger. Soon it was chirping non-stop, loud and urgent. It filled the kitchen with sound.

Kevin's father heard it from the lounge. He turned off the Super 12 on Sky and came in. Kevin explained what had happened. "Noisy devil," said his father. He swept under the dishwasher with the fly-swatter.

He couldn't bring it out, and after a few seconds it started chirping again. "Where's that fly-spray?" he said.

Kevin remembered the feel of its legs scrabbling against his hands. He suddenly wanted it to live. "Why kill it, Dad?"

His father looked at him in astonishment. "Because it'll chirp all day and all night, Son, that's why. Drive us mad. And it's not going to get a mate from there, even if it chirps its guts out. Probably die soon, anyway. Usually do at the end of autumn. Doing it a favour."

Kevin thought of a solution. "We could take the dishwasher out."

"No!" said his father sharply. "Pipes and all sorts back there. It's just a cricket, Son. If it's still chirping in the morning, too bad — it's the gas chamber." Kevin opened his mouth. "No!" said his father again. "I'm too tired to argue."

Kevin went to bed, but he couldn't sleep. He heard the cricket calling for a mate that would never hear it and never come. No future for you in there, Chirpy, he thought.

Kevin thought of a plan. He waited until his dad had gone to bed in the other bedroom and would be well asleep. Then he took his small camping torch and crept quietly down the stairs.

Once he was in the kitchen, he put his torch on the floor. Then he began to wriggle the dishwasher out of its cubbyhole, bit by bit. Once it was out, he'd grab Chirpy and put him outside. Simple — provided Dad didn't wake.

He didn't get far. A torch beam shone into his face, blinding him. "Stay where you are!" yelled a voice. "Hands above your head!"

The kitchen light flashed on. "Kevin!" said his father. "I came down here and saw this torch and I guess I thought you were a bur—" His voice faltered. A small silence. "I told you not to shift the dishwasher," he said.

Kevin looked at his father. He realised he'd come down because he was going to squirt the fly-spray in the middle of the night, without him knowing. "You said you were going to wait till morning," he said, accusingly.

His father sighed. "I did." He shrugged his shoulders. "Okay," he said. "Let's pull out the dishwasher."

It was out in a couple of minutes. The cricket, frightened and covered in dust, was trying to be invisible in a corner.

This time, Kevin's cupped hands held it tight. His dad

opened the door and Kevin went out into the cool night. He opened his hands. For a moment, the cricket stayed still, as if it couldn't believe its luck. Then it jumped. A tiny rustle in the darkness and it was gone.

Kevin went back into the kitchen. His dad had already shoved the dishwasher back. "A hard day's work tomorrow — and you've got school," he said. "Time for bed."

Suddenly he came over to Kevin and gave him an awkward hug. "Proud of you, Kev," he said. He went upstairs.

Before Kevin went to bed, he leaned out his window. The stars were shining and there was dew in the air. Then he heard a shrill noise start up, right where he'd let the cricket go. Kevin couldn't stop grinning. Good on you, Chirpy, he thought.

21

The Rat and the Little Black Scaup

James Norcliffe

One day, as Little Black Scaup dibbled in the waters of Horseshoe Lake with her three little black ducklings, she saw a very strange sight. There seemed to be a lump in the water, travelling quickly over the surface. She looked again and it was heading straight towards her. It had no neck. No feathers. It certainly wasn't a bird.

She felt uncomfortable — so much so she called her little ones and paddled quickly to one side to get out of its way. She half expected the lump to change direction and veer towards them, but it did not. It just kept travelling in the same direction in a very straight line.

When it reached her side of the lake it didn't stop. Something lumpy broke the surface and scurried right up the little sandy shore and on to the land. It stood there for a moment shaking violently. Little diamonds of water were flung into the air and the wet, slicked-down fur suddenly became spiky.

It was a rat. A very wet black rat.

The rat stopped shaking and turned about, lifting its head into the air and sniffing.

Suddenly the rat noticed Little Black Scaup and the ducklings and said, "What are you staring at, ducks?"

The scaup was embarrassed. She hadn't really been staring. She had just been curious.

She said, "I'm sorry. I didn't know what you were or what you were doing. I've never seen a rat swimming like that before."

The rat grinned, baring his sharp little yellow teeth. "I'm in training."

"In training?"

"For the Horseshoe Lake Speed Swimming Champion-ships. I mean to be the fastest rat on the water."

Little Black Scaup was impressed. "Goodness," she said.

"I want the blue ribbon," said the rat. He glanced at the ducklings, then gave Little Black Scaup a crafty little smile. "You know," he said. "You could help me if you like."

"Could I?" said Little Black Scaup. She rather liked the idea of helping others.

"Well," said the rat, "I have a big problem. I know I'm going pretty fast. But I have no idea just how fast . . ."

Little Black Scaup nodded.

"You see," explained the rat. "I need somebody to time me."

"I see," said Little Black Scaup. "How could I do that?"

The rat grinned again. "It's very easy," he said. "We, that's you and me, we'll swim together over to the other side of the lake. You say *Go!* and start counting and I'll swim as fast as I can back over here to your little ones. When I reach them you can tell me what number you're up to."

Little Black Scaup nodded. "That seems easy enough."

"Good." The rat clapped his front paws and grinned again. "Let's go!"

"Wait here for Mr Rat, little ones," said Little Black Scaup. And she paddled across the lake to the other side while the rat burrowed through the water beside her in his clumsy, lumpish way.

Meanwhile, Auntie Shag had been sitting motionless on a stump not far away. She had neither opened her eyes nor moved a muscle, but she had heard everything that was said. She opened her eyes now, and watched Little Black Scaup and the rat make their way across the lake. Once they were out of hearing, she called softly to the three little ducklings. "Swim away, little ones. Hide under the bank somewhere well away from here."

"But . . ." said the biggest little duckling.

"Do as I say at once!" said Auntie Shag in such a stern voice that the ducklings scurried off to hide without another murmur.

Shortly afterwards, Little Black Scaup and the rat reached the other side of the lake. Auntie Shag heard Little Black Scaup cry "*Go!*" and begin counting: *One. Two. Three. Four* . . . As Little Black Scaup counted, Auntie Shag saw the little lump that was the rat move steadily towards her. He really was swimming very quickly. Closer and closer came the fast-moving lump. Just before he reached the other side though, he stopped swimming and poked his head out of the water, moving it back and forth with his fixed yellow grin. Suddenly the grin faded as he realised that the ducklings had vanished.

"Where's my lunch?" he demanded in an angry whine. Treading water, he glared up at Auntie Shag. "Where's my lunch, shag? Have you got them?"

"I haven't got your lunch, Mr Rat," said Auntie Shag lazily, "but I'm thinking that perhaps you might have mine!"

At that, the shag dived off the stump and disappeared into the lake.

"Where's she gone? Where's she gone?" asked the rat, worried.

He didn't have to wait long to find out. Auntie Shag emerged from the water just behind the surprised rat, his tail gripped in her long beak.

"Hey!" cried the rat.

The shag didn't reply. She couldn't have replied even if she'd wanted to, as her beak was tightly closed on the rat's tail.

"Hey!" cried the rat again as Auntie Shag launched into the air and

flew up into the uppermost branches of a nearby ribbonwood tree.

Meanwhile, over on the other side of the lake Little Black Scaup was still counting *Twenty-six. Twenty-seven. Twenty-eight . . .* She stopped when she realised that instead of swimming across the lake, Mr Rat was now swinging like a squealing pendulum from the beak of Auntie Shag, thirty metres up in the air.

"Goodness," she said, as Auntie Shag left the tree and flew even higher into the air.

"Hey! Hey! Hey!" cried the rat.

Then the Auntie Shag opened her beak and let the rat go. Down, down the rat fell, squealing and waving his legs helplessly, down, down until he hit the water with a loud splosh.

"Goodness," said Little Black Scaup again. "I hadn't realised that Mr Rat was training for the high-diving championship as well. What an amazing sportsman he must be."

"I couldn't agree more," laughed Auntie Shag as she came down to land beside her. "But hadn't you better go and find your ducklings? They'll be wondering where you are."

"I think I should," said Little Black Scaup. "There are some nasty characters about, I've been told."

And she set off back across the lake.

22

Fair Shares

David Hill

At breakfast, Tyron saw two terrifying things. First, there was hardly any peanut butter left in the jar. Second, his twin sister Tania was reaching for it.

Tyron glared and grabbed at the jar. Tania glared and grabbed too. CLATTER! The jar fell over and rolled across the table. CRASH! It hit the kitchen floor and broke into six pieces.

"Aw, Tyron!" went Tania.

"Aw, Tania!" went Tyron.

"Are you two having a smashing time?" their dad asked. "Slow down, please. Try giving, not grabbing, Okay?"

"Okay," said Tania. She poked out her tongue at Tyron.

"Okay," said Tyron. He crossed his eyes at Tania.

Their father saw them. "All right," he said. "Tania, go and stack the dishes. Tyron, go and take out the rubbish. That'll give you both time to think."

Tyron stamped down the back steps. Missy the cat

crouched on the lawn nearby. "Get out of my way!" Tyron hissed at her.

His skateboard lay on the path nearby. Tyron gave it a kick that sent it somersaulting towards the flax bush by the gate. Missy jumped.

Then Tyron jumped, too. A shrill *Tchick-Tchick! Tchick-Tchick!* sounded from the flax bush, and a small shape flashed out. It swerved as it saw Tyron, banged into the skateboard, and fluttered to the ground.

Tyron started towards the bird. Too slow — there was a grey blur in front of him, and Missy had it in her mouth. She turned like a snake, ears back and body flattened close to the lawn, looking for a way past Tyron.

"No, Missy! Stay!" Tyron spread his arms wide and took three quick steps forward, blocking the cat's escape. Missy drew back towards the flax bush. Above the wad of feathers in her mouth, her yellow eyes glared at Tyron. The bird lay still. Only its beak opened and closed slowly.

Tyron moved towards the crouching cat. "Give it here, Missy. Give!" That's the second time today some annoying female has grabbed something I want, he thought.

Missy backed further towards the bush. Her tail flicked. Tyron could see now that the bird was a thrush. It lay upside-down in the cat's jaws, its speckled white throat and fawn breast towards the sky. One dark-brown wing was folded flat along its body, the other stuck out the side of Missy's mouth.

Maybe if I give her a fright she'll let it go, Tyron thought. 'YAHHHH!" he yelled suddenly. Missy sprang back till she was right up against the flax bush. Her head was sunk down into her shoulders, and her ears flattened along her skull. Her pupils were black slits. The thrush's own bright black eye stared at Tyron.

Tyron bent forward, and began waving his left hand slowly from side to side. The cat's head turned as she followed the movement. Then Tyron's right hand shot forward and grabbed Missy by the neck. She hunched and pulled against him, but he held her firm.

"Right," he muttered at her. "I'll have that, thanks." Still holding the cat's quivering neck with his right hand, he started working at Missy's mouth with his left, trying to force her jaws open.

He couldn't move them. Not without jamming his fingers inside and crushing the thrush. Each time he lifted the corner of Missy's mouth, uncovering the pink gums and white daggers of teeth, he could feel her clench a bit harder. Her eyes glared at him. She looks just like stupid Tania, Tyron thought to himself.

"Let it go!" Tyron hissed at her. "You stupid cat! Let it go!"

Then Tyron went still. What had his dad said to him? "Slow down . . . Try giving, not grabbing."

"Stay!" Tyron went again, and hurried inside. Half a minute later, he was back again, holding a saucer of milk in one hand and a dish of cat food in the other. Missy still crouched on the lawn. The bird hung unmoving in her mouth.

"Here, Missy." Tyron was calling softly to the cat now, not yelling at her like before. "Here, girl."

He put the saucer of milk down on the lawn, dipped a finger in it and held the finger out to the cat. "Something to drink with no nasty feathers in it," he told her. Missy stared.

Tyron put the dish of cat food down beside the milk. "And something to eat with no nasty beaks in it," he said. Missy stared harder. Her whiskers puffed around the thrush.

"Smell, Missie!" Tyron put his finger in the cat food and held it near Missy. The cat's nose twitched. "Something with no nasty claws in it, either," he said. The cat sniffed. Her nose was twitching so hard now that it seemed about to fall off. But she still held onto the thrush.

"Last chance, Missy," Tyron murmured. He began slowly pulling the milk and cat food away from her. Centimetre by centimetre, further and further.

Then Missy moved. Suddenly, so suddenly that Tyron blinked, she dropped the thrush, flowed forward, and started gobbling at the cat food.

Tyron scooped up the cat with one hand and the cat food with his other hand. He ran with them both back into the house, put them down on the hall floor and shut the door on them. He rushed back to the lawn, just in time to see something brown and speckled flutter up to the top of the fence and away into the sky.

"How about saying thank you?" Tyron called after it.

Back in the house, Missy had eaten all the cat food and drunk half the milk. She looked around, and Tyron thought she was going to ask "Hey? Where's my bird?" but she started washing herself instead.

"See," his dad said, after Tyron told him what had happened. "Giving is better than grabbing."

"It works with cats," Tyron said. "Does it works with twin sisters?"

His father looked surprised. Then he laughed. "Don't see why not."

Tyron stood up, and headed for Tania's room.

"Tania?" he called. "Here, Tania, Tania, Tania! Your nice brother's got something just for you! He's got you a lovely saucer of milk and a yummy dish of cat food!"

23

The Scribbily Scrabbily Dinosaur

Alan Bagnall

The warm morning sun is shining deep into Room Six. Our sliding doors are wide open. We are all busy, heads down, writing stories.

Suddenly Chantelle calls out, "Oh, look! Look! Look out on the veranda!"

With a scrape and a clatter, everyone stands and squints into the sun. A monstrous lizard-like creature has strolled onto our veranda! It must be nearly five metres long!

"Sit down everyone! Sit down!" Miss Chalmers orders. She's about to shout, "Get under your desks!" when she realises this is not an earthquake. This is only an old dinosaur; most likely a very old dinosaur.

"It's got scribbily scrabbily skin," Rosa says to herself as she sits down. She quickly writes "scribbily scrabbily skin" into her dinosaur story. The dinosaur stretches out, lies down and rests its head on its paws.

Room Six falls silent. The dinosaur begins to snore gently.

"Oh dear!" Miss Chalmers sighs. "How am I supposed to handle a dinosaur? I missed the course on dinosaur handling. It was held during our concert week."

"Please, Miss!" Kurei calls out. "Shall I get Mr Wilson?" Miss Chalmers heaves another great sigh and nods.

Kurei races off and soon returns with Mr Wilson. Mr Wilson is able to put his gloves on and clean up yucky messes that ordinary people don't even want to look at. He knows how to manage all sorts of things. Sometimes he can even make a soccer ball roll off the roof by whistling to it.

Mr Wilson strides around the sleeping dinosaur. He takes his gloves off and touches it. "It's got beautiful scribbily scrabbily skin, Miss Chalmers!" he says. Rosa smiles and writes three more sentences. "But I can't handle this dinosaur on my own!" Mr Wilson decides. "I'll need help. Many hands make light work, you know."

Miss Chalmers sighs again. "Please don't wake it up," she whispers.

"Right!" Mr Wilson orders. "Gather round, guys! We'll need twelve helpers on each side! Boy, girl; boy, girl; we don't want the girls taking all the weight, do we? I'll manage the jaws. Will you carry the tail, Miss Chalmers? Now, each of you put a hand gently under this dinosaur and when I say, we'll all lift together: Ready, steady, LIFT!"

Rosa smiles a satisfied smile. She can feel the dinosaur's scribbily scrabbily skin. And with everyone helping, it really isn't too heavy.

Mr Wilson cradles the jaws in his arms and we all follow him across the playground, carrying the sleeping dinosaur. We put it gently down in the shade of the pohutukawa trees and return to story writing. Our stories are getting better and better.

Finally Jared looks at the clock and waves his hand, "Please, Miss! It's past playtime!"

Chantelle has finished her story too. "Look!" she calls out. "Look outside! The dinosaur has woken up! It's crawling under the old dental clinic! It's probably been living there for millions of years!"

24

The Butterfly

Dianne Hogan

There was a chrysalis on the swan plant. It was bright green with a circle of gold. Every day Jennifer hoped the chrysalis would open. She couldn't wait to see the monarch butterfly inside. You could see the shape of its wings now. That meant it was almost time.

Before the chrysalis, there had been a fat black and yellow caterpillar nibbling at the leaves of the swan plant. Then the caterpillar had hung from a branch and shed its skin, and the new skin of the chrysalis had grown over it.

One day her father called, "Jenny, Ben. The butterfly has come out."

Jennifer and her little brother Ben ran across the lawn to see the butterfly holding onto the split chrysalis with its legs. Jennifer thought it was the brightest orange colour and the deepest black she had ever seen.

"No wonder they're called monarch, king of the butterflies," said her mother, who had come to look as well.

"When will it fly?" asked Ben.

"When its wings are dry," said their father, "in about a day. I hope the wasps don't get it."

"Would they, Dad?" asked Jennifer.

"They could. Mr Mackie said they attack butterflies."

Jennifer knew it must be true if Mr Mackie said so. He had lots of swan plants. Butterflies were his hobby. "I hate wasps," she said.

They had only bought the swan plant three weeks ago. Then the wasps had come. Dozens and dozens of them, zipping here and there, and coming into the house. Both Jennifer and Ben had been stung.

Their father said the wasps that year were a plague. Their mother had put some juice and honey in a bottle outside. It had trapped a lot of wasps, but there were far too many to make much difference.

Jennifer kept checking on the butterfly, and shooed away any wasps that came near, with a feathery branch from the wattle tree. Her father said he would keep an eye on the monarch, while Jennifer was having her lunch.

Jennifer was eating a sandwich in the kitchen when Ben came running in. "Jenny, Jenny, a wasp got the butterfly."

Jennifer ran outside to see her father crouched in the garden. "Dad," she said, "where is the butterfly?"

"Down here," said her father. "It happened so fast."

Jennifer saw the monarch lying on the ground. "Is it

dead?" she asked sadly.

"I'm not sure," said her father.

There were tears in Jennifer's eyes as she gently laid the butterfly on her palm. Then she saw its wings flutter. "It's alive!" she said. Jennifer took the butterfly inside and put it on a windowsill in the bathroom.

The next day when she came home from school, she hurried inside. "Mum," she said, "How is the butterfly?"

"Go and see," said her mother.

Jennifer went to the bathroom, and there was the monarch, upright now and stretching its wings. Jennifer smiled. She had been worried about it all day.

Later when Jennifer's father came home, he said, "I was talking to Mr Mackie today. He said the butterfly needs flowers. It sucks the nectar from them for its food."

Jennifer cut a long branch with flowers from the swan plant. She placed the branch in a jar of water. Then she put her hand close to the butterfly and it walked easily across her fingers.

"Can I have a turn?" Ben asked.

Jennifer put her arm next to Ben's and the butterfly walked onto his hand.

"That tickles," said Ben, laughing.

The butterfly stretched its wings very wide for the first time.

"Wow," said Ben.

"Isn't it lovely," said Jennifer. Then she put the monarch on the branch and they watched it search out nectar from the flowers with its long tongue.

The next day, the butterfly was flitting around the bathroom window as if it wanted to get out.

"I think it's ready to fly. You can't keep it in the bathroom for ever, Jen," said her mother.

At dusk, when the wasps had gone from the garden, Jennifer put the butterfly outside.

The following morning, Jennifer was up early. She went outside. The monarch was where she had left it, on the swan plant. "I'd fly away if I were you, butterfly," she said, "before the wasps wake up."

Jennifer held the butterfly in her palm. It flexed its wings, then flew from her hand — but only a short way — and landed on a low bush. Jennifer tried again, three times, lifting her hands in the air to get the butterfly airborne. But the same thing happened. "Dad," she called to her father, "what can we do? The monarch won't fly away."

Jennifer's father walked over and looked closely at the butterfly. "There's a nip out of its wing — on the tip, see. That must be where the wasp got it."

"Does that mean it will never fly?" asked Jennifer.

"Perhaps not very far," said her father.

Jennifer thought for a moment. Then she said, "I'll take it to school. There are a lot of butterflies there, and not nearly as many wasps."

School was half an hour's drive away. Jennifer put the butterfly in a box with holes in the top for air. She held it on her lap all the way in the car.

Outside Room Eight, Jennifer opened the box and put the butterfly on a bushy swan plant. "There's plenty here for you to eat," she said.

Morning lessons seemed to go on forever. When the bell rang for playtime, Jennifer was first out the door.

There were a lot of monarchs on the plant, but after a while Jennifer saw her butterfly with the tiny piece off its wing. It hopped from one plant to another, feeding on the flowers.

Jennifer was happy she had brought the butterfly to school. It would be all right now.

25

The Last Horses

Jane Buxton

My brother and I loved to play in the long grass that grew along the roadside outside our house. We'd wriggle through it on our stomachs, creeping up on each other, or we'd pretend to be tigers stalking through the jungle. It was a wonderful place to play.

But, several times a year, a mower would come to cut the grass. The mower was pulled by two huge horses called Bessie and Punch.

When Andrew and I heard the clip-clop-clip-clop of their hooves on the road, we'd run inside shouting to Mum, "The horses are coming! The mower is here! Quick, Mum! We need apples! Is there any spare bread?"

"Put your shoes on first," Mum would always say. "If those horses tread on you with their great hooves . . ."

But we never had time to stop for our shoes. We'd grab the apples or bread and race out to the gate.

The man who drove the horses wouldn't let us near

while they were working. It was too dangerous. We'd hang over the gate and watch the long blade cutting and the grass falling in a wide green sheet. It took only a few minutes.

"Whoa there, Bessie. Whoa, Punch," the mower man would say. "Time for refreshments. Let's see what these kiddies have got for you."

Then we would climb down from the gate to feed the horses.

"Talk to them so they know you're coming up behind them," the mower man said. "They can't see you with their blinkers on."

"Good girl, Bessie. It's all right, Punch. It's only us."

"That's right," said the mower man. "Now hold your hand out flat with the apple in the middle. That way they won't get your fingers by mistake."

The horses were huge. Their necks and shoulders were wet with sweat. They leaned their big heads over us, breathing hard from their work. But their eyes were kind. The bits clinked in their mouths as they took the bread and apples gently between their soft, whiskery lips.

"Watch out for your toes!" said Mum from the gate. "Don't stand so close." But Bessie and Punch never moved until we were safely out of the way and the mower man shouted, "Hey-up!" and clicked his tongue.

As soon as the horses moved off, my brother would dive into the cut grass, rolling and playing and making it into heaps. But I always ran to the corner and watched till the horses were out of sight.

Then, one summer, the horses didn't come. The grass

along the roadside grew tall and started to go to seed.

"Time those council horses came to cut the grass," said Dad. But instead there came a noisy red tractor pulling a different mower behind it.

"Where are the horses?" we shouted from the gate. But the man on the tractor just waved and smiled. He couldn't hear us. We watched until the grass lay in a flat green sea on the roadside and the tractor drove off around the corner.

"Shall we make a hut in it?" said Andrew. But the roadside didn't seem the same any more. We had one grass fight and then went inside.

"It's the end of an era," Dad said when we told him. "I'll miss those horses. That must have been the last horse-drawn machine still working for the council."

"They were old," I said. "The man told us Bessie was twenty-three. And that was last year."

"Yes, that is old," said Mum. "They've most likely been retired to the country."

"Or made into pet food," said Dad. "It costs money to keep old horses."

"Raymond," said Mum. "Don't tease."

But I knew Dad was probably right. I was sure we'd never see Bessie and Punch again.

On the last Saturday of the summer holidays, we all went for a drive to an orchard to pick our own apples. On the way home Dad decided to drive through the back roads for a change. The car bumped along hot, dusty roads. Andrew fell asleep and I stared out the window, trying not to feel carsick.

Then, all of a sudden I saw them — a black horse and a chestnut horse, so big and so strong-looking I was sure they were the mower horses.

"Stop the car!" I shouted, thumping on the back of Dad's seat.

"Don't frighten me!" growled Dad. "You'll cause an accident."

"Could we turn and go back?" I asked in a small voice. But I knew Dad couldn't stop on that narrow road with another car behind us.

We never went back along that road again, so I could never be sure whether the two big horses were Bessie and Punch. Their paddock was lush with clover and green grass; they were standing under willow trees by a lovely stream.

I'd like to think it was them.

26

Ms Winsley and the Incognito TV Star

Barbara Else

Ms Winsley wore her paisley party-dress. She sat in the motel restaurant and looked at the menu. The parrots in the palm trees squawked outside. "Polly wants a cracker," they cried.

"I need much more than a cracker," Ms Winsley said. "I'm starved. This is the last night of my holiday and I deserve a feast. Prawns in golden syrup? That sounds great." She licked her lips. "No. Goose eggs in green sauce for me."

She looked for a waiter, but they were all clustered at the doorway. "You can't bring that in here! Quick! Fetch the manager!" one cried.

The manager dashed over to the door and stood there with his arms crossed. He began to argue with someone.

"Not in my dining room," the manager said. "Go away."

Ms Winsley craned her neck to see who wasn't allowed

in the dining room. It was a woman in a dull grey dress with a tatty brown bow on the shoulder. She looked nearly as boring as a Prime Minister. She was very, very thin, and Ms Winsley thought that she needed a good big feed.

What could the problem be? But Ms Winsley was on holiday. She was not here to help people out of tricky situations. She had to have a break.

She looked back at the menu. Brussels sprouts in kumara jelly, she read. "Mega yummy!" said Ms Winsley.

"But I'm hungry!" said the woman at the door. "So hungry I could eat a horse!"

"We've only got buffalo today," the manager said.

Ms Winsley shouldn't try to help. She couldn't, wouldn't, shouldn't. But she couldn't bear it any longer. "Excuse me," she called out. "Do you have a problem?"

"No," said the waiters.

"No," said the manager and stalked off.

'Yes,' said the woman in the dull grey dress.

Ms Winsley pushed back her chair and strode across to help. "My job is fixing problems. I run Tricky Situation Services. You've probably heard of it."

"For sure," said the woman. "Ms Winsley to the rescue. What a heroine you are."

"This woman can't come in," the waiters said. "She's not dressed properly."

"It's a dress," said the woman. "I'm on holiday."

"A dull grey dress, on holiday?" said Ms Winsley. She looked closely at the woman. "I think I know you," she said. "Usually you wear a tiara. Either you're a TV star, or else you're a member of the Royal Family."

"Right first time," said the TV star.

"This is Glory-Anna the Gorgeous!" Ms Winsley told the waiters. "She's the woman with a thousand faces. Soap operas. She's the biggest star of all."

"But I'm travelling incognito," said Glory-Anna.

"What's incognito?" asked a waiter.

"Nobody's meant to guess," Ms Winsley said.

"You did," said the waiter. "Anyway she still can't come in here." He went to shut the door in Glory-Anna's gorgeous face. Ms Winsley stuck her foot in the doorway.

"She's hungry, and she's skinny as a flea. You have to let her in."

The waiters turned pale and trembled. "It's her sp—sp— sp— " they spluttered.

"My spider?" cried Glory-Anna. She stroked the bow on her shoulder. "But TV stars are meant to have strange pets."

Ms Winsley looked more closely at the dull grey dress. The brown bow was not made of ribbon at all. It had legs. Eight legs. A big brown tarantula perched upon Glory-Anna's shoulder.

"Amanda wouldn't hurt a fly," said the TV star.

"Are you scared of spiders?" Ms Winsley asked the waiters.

"Isn't everyone?" they said.

"I'm not," said Ms Winsley.

"I don't care how famous and clever she is. The manager said nobody with a sp—sp— *that,* is going to come inside," announced a waiter.

Ms Winsley took Glory-Anna's skinny arm and they went into the garden.

"Can't you leave your spider in your room?" Ms Winsley asked.

Tears made spots upon the dull grey dress. "Amanda gets lonely," Glory-Anna said. "So do I. It's awful to be beautiful and famous, because nobody loves you for yourself alone. Amanda is the only one I trust to love me truly."

"You can't get by without your dinner, though," Ms Winsley said.

The TV star stuck her chin in the air. "I'd rather starve than leave Amanda all alone."

"I've seen tricky situations before," Ms Winsley said. "This won't beat me." She folded her arms so she could think.

Glory-Anna gave the spider little kisses. The spider kissed her too.

"Can Amanda act? Is she a soap-opera star like you?" Ms Winsley asked.

"She's a spider," said Glory-Anna. "But she's watched me act."

"And have you brought amazing make-up with you?" asked Ms Winsley.

"I don't leave home without it," Glory-Anna said.

"A spangly dress?"

"Of course."

They went to the TV star's motel room.

"Put on your brightest dress," Ms Winsley said. "And may I hold the spider?"

"Her name's Amanda," said the TV star. She handed the spider to Ms Winsley, and went to rummage in the wardrobe.

"Sit still, Amanda," said Ms Winsley. "I'll fix this in a jiffy."

She held Amanda carefully, chose some silver eye shadow and painted Amanda's eight hairy legs with it. With gold eyeliner, she painted Amanda's fat little body. Amanda glowed and sparkled.

"How's this?" asked Glory-Anna. She did a twirl, in a red gown covered in sequins.

"Lovely," said Ms Winsley. "Now we'll put on your tiara." Ms Winsley arranged Amanda on top of Glory-Anna's head.

The spider made a charming sight. It was perfect with the bright red spangly gown.

"Stay," said Ms Winsley to Amanda. "Don't move till after dinner."

At the dining room door, the waiters looked at Glory-Anna with great suspicion. Ms Winsley's heart thumped like anything. But Amanda was an excellent actor. She stayed still, just as a tiara should.

Ms Winsley and Glory-Anna sat down and looked at the menu.

"Broccoli stew?" asked the TV star.

"Yuck," said Ms Winsley. "Turtle pie, with walnut stuffing?"

Glory-Anna made one of her thousand faces.

A waiter came to take their order. He looked admiringly at the bright red dress, and uneasily at the tiara.

Just then, a fly flew in the window. Ms Winsley could hardly breathe for fright. What if Amanda couldn't contain herself? What if she jumped to catch the fly? Mind you,

Glory-Anna had said Amanda wouldn't hurt a . . .

"Stay!" Ms Winsley whispered anyway. "Stay, Amanda! Stay!"

"Fish and chips," she said out loud. "Two helpings, thanks, and make them big ones."

And Amanda waited till the waiter had gone, before she jumped and caught *her* dinner. So much for not hurting a fly — but we all get hungry sometimes.

"How can I thank you?" asked Glory-Anna.

"Forget it," said Ms Winsley. "I might need your help one day."

"Ms Winsley, you're terrific!" said the TV star.

The parrots in the palm trees laughed and squawked, and teased the kangaroos in the mango patch. And finally, Ms Winsley and Glory-Anna ate their dinner. It was the last night of her holiday — Ms Winsley was feasting with a star! — and every chip was perfect, fat and hot.

27

Operation 'Dog'

Maria Gill

Sniff, sniff. I know that pine smell — I've smelt it before.
Sniff — I can smell some other dogs. Twitch. I can hear a
cat making a fuss. Oh no! I'm at the vet's.

I'm not going with the nurse.

Where is she taking me? It's so white and shiny in here.
I'm not going in that cage. You're going to have to force me
in . . .

I'm in the cage with barely room to turn around. I'll
flutter my eyes at her with a 'get-me-out-of-here' look; that
usually works.

I've been waiting ages. Is that a needle she's holding?
She'd better not poke it in me. Ouch! That hurt. I'll leap
out of the cage . . . just after . . . I've had a nap. I feel so
sleepy — snoooore . . .

Nelson is carried to an operating table and laid down on
his back. He has a lump on his stomach that they want to

take out to see if it is diseased.

Now he's asleep, he looks like he's frozen in time. His tongue hangs out of his mouth like a drooping pink petal. The nurse attaches a mask over Nelson's nose to help him breathe and connects him to a machine that beeps every time his heart beats. Competing with the beeps are birds cheeping outside and a radio blaring in the other room. The nurse checks the machine every five minutes to see that Nelson is sleeping and not in any danger.

The vet washes his hands while the nurse lays out the tools on a blue cloth on a silver trolley. She shaves Nelson's stomach and wipes it clean.

The winter sun provides plenty of light in the room when the vet walks in. He clips a blue sheet over the dog's body and sits down on a stool beside the operating table. He picks up a knife and cuts through Nelson's stomach as if cutting through leather. Different tools cut, poke and stitch Nelson's insides as the vet takes out the lump and lays it on the blue cloth. It lies there, pink and wet-looking. He stitches the skin together and the blood is wiped off.

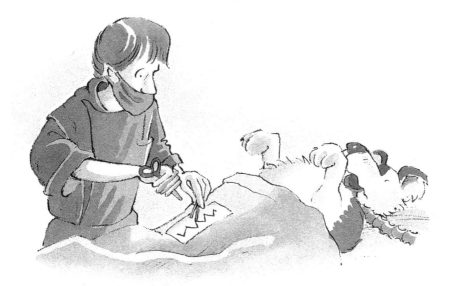

Nelson remains on the operating table until he is breathing by himself. The mask and heart machine are removed and he is carried back to his cage. The nurse checks on him regularly to see if he is getting better.

Sniff, sniff. Still that pine smell. Now where am I? That's right — the vet's. How long am I going to be stuck in this cage? I'm not going to let anyone touch me.

My legs aren't right; they're all wobbly. Ouch! It hurts when I move. I've got a zipper on my skin — how did it get there?

Here's my owner — come to pick me up. Woof — it wasn't too bad — woof! Let's go home — woof!

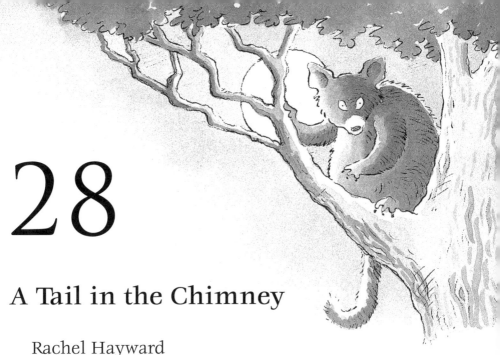

28

A Tail in the Chimney

Rachel Hayward

When Tim came home from school on Monday, there was a tail sticking out of the chimney. It was grey, and very bushy.

Grandad was standing in the front garden, talking to Mrs Fyfe-Palmer from next door.

"It's a disgrace!" Mrs Fyfe-Palmer said. "We never had problems with rodents until you people arrived!" She marched into her house, slamming the front door behind her.

"What's up?" Tim asked.

"A possum," said Grandad, pointing. "In our chimney. Mrs F-P is not pleased."

As Tim watched, the tail disappeared, and a moment later a small, furry face popped up. "It's cute!" Tim said. "Maybe we could keep it?"

Grandad shook his head. "Possums are trouble. Before you know it, it'll nip the tops off the roses, and invite its mates around for a party. I'll get rid of it tomorrow."

Tim didn't like to ask what Grandad was going to do. He went to bed thinking about the possum's little face, and feeling sad.

In the middle of the night, Tim sat bolt upright in bed, his heart pounding. There was a terrible snorting, rattly, gasping noise outside his window. He pulled back the curtains and peeked cautiously out. The possum was perched on the fence, its eyes glittering in the light from the porch.

Grandad came into Tim's room. "Up to its tricks already, is it?" he asked. "I'll pop out and have a word with it."

A moment or two later, Grandad appeared outside the window. He looked up at the possum, and said something in a gruff, scritchy voice, in a language Tim couldn't understand. The possum looked startled. It sprang lightly along the top of the fence, and disappeared into the darkness.

"What did you say?" Tim asked, when Grandad came back inside.

"I said it should find something better to do than waking people up. Get a hobby of some sort," said Grandad, tucking Tim in. "It's gone off to think about it. Go to sleep now."

Tim lay awake for a long time, wondering.

At breakfast, Tim said to Mum, "I think Grandad's a possum whisperer."

"A what?" laughed Mum.

"He can talk to possums," explained Tim. "Make them do things."

Before Mum could answer, there was a sharp rap on the back door. Dad opened it to find Mrs Fyfe-Palmer waiting on the doorstep.

"Rodents," said Mrs Fyfe-Palmer. "*Pests*! This is a very good neighbourhood, and you are *lowering the tone*." She leaned in close and peered into Dad's face. "What are you planning to do about it?"

"About what?" asked Dad blankly.

"That possum!" shouted Mrs Fyfe-Palmer. She grabbed Dad by his dressing-gown cord, dragged him out into the garden, and pointed up. The possum's tail stuck up like a flag in the chimney.

"I'll call someone," said Dad faintly. "Soon. Or now," he said, as Mrs Fyfe-Palmer glowered at him.

When Tim came home from school, there was a van parked in the driveway. The sign on the side read 'Pests Away'. There was a man by the front gate, talking to Mrs Fyfe-Palmer. "I've put the trap in the bushes," he explained. "He goes in, grabs the apple and BANG! The door shuts on him."

Grandad was drinking tea in the kitchen. When Tim told him about the pest man, he just smiled and poured some tea into his saucer to cool. "My money's on the possum," he said.

In the middle of the night, Tim woke to a terrible bashing and crashing above his head. He got his torch and went outside. Grandad was leaning against the fence in his pyjamas, watching the possum prance across the roof, spinning wildly. It was eating an apple.

Mum and Dad rushed outside, tousled and wild-eyed.

"What's it doing?" asked Mum, aghast.

"I think it's dancing," said Grandad. "It's my fault — I suggested it take up a hobby."

Mum and Dad stared at him.

"I told you he can talk to possums," said Tim.

"Don't be so ridiculous!" said Dad.

An apple core sailed down from the roof and bounced off Dad's head.

As Tim went to bed, he heard Grandad speaking in the mysterious, guttural voice out by the fence. When he came back inside, Tim hissed, "Grandad! What did you say this time?"

Grandad poked his head around the bedroom door. "I said maybe Scottish country dancing wasn't the best hobby for a possum – he should choose something quieter."

"Like what?" asked Tim.

"Chess, maybe," said Grandad. "Or stamp collecting. Go to sleep now."

When Tim came home from school the next day, he could hear Mrs Fyfe-Palmer shouting before he got halfway down their street. She was at her mailbox, waving a handful of letters at Grandad.

"Those are tooth marks! That creature is eating my mail!" She

flourished an envelope. "If it's ruined the tickets for my South Pacific cruise, I'll be expecting you people to pay for them!"

Grandad nodded at Mrs Fyfe-Palmer, smiled politely, then went back to pruning the roses. Mrs Fyfe-Palmer snorted in disgust and stomped inside. Grandad winked at Tim.

"Seems our possum took my advice," he said. He held out a handful of their own letters, all with the corners nibbled off. "Same thing all up and down the street. It's started collecting stamps. I'd better have another word."

That night, Tim peeked from behind the curtains while Grandad spoke to the possum. At last the possum leapt up and away into a clump of cabbage trees. Grandad stood in the garden for a little bit longer, smoking his pipe and smiling quietly to himself.

For the next few days, there was no sign of the possum. Grandad wouldn't tell Tim what he'd said to it. Whenever Tim asked, he tapped the side of his nose mysteriously.

On Sunday, Mrs Fyfe-Palmer left for her South Pacific cruise. Tim swung on the gate, watching as the taxi driver struggled out to the taxi with one suitcase after another. There was so much luggage, he had to tie some of it on the roof of the car. Mrs Fyfe-Palmer stood on the footpath, giving instructions. As the driver loaded the last of the bags, she turned and looked back at Tim and Grandad.

"I see that dreadful beast is gone," she said, looking up at the chimney with a delicate shudder. "Poison, I suppose? Or a trap?"

Grandad shook his head. "I just suggested a new hobby," he said cheerfully. "The rest took care of itself."

Mrs Fyfe-Palmer glared at him. "Nonsense," she snapped. She climbed into the taxi, and barked at the driver, "Take me to the wharf!"

As the taxi pulled away, Tim caught sight of something strange poking out of one of Mrs Fyfe-Palmer's bags on the roof of the car. Something grey, and very bushy.

"Grandad," he said slowly, "what hobby did you suggest to the possum this time?"

"International travel," said Grandad, with a grin. "I hear the South Pacific's very nice this time of year."

The possum's tail waved in the breeze, as Mrs Fyfe-Palmer's taxi rounded the corner, and drove off towards the wharf.

29

Winnie Weta's Scary Adventure with the Child-People

Jan Thorburn

Once upon a time, not so very long ago, there lived a family of wetas in the old karaka tree that grew next to the postman's house. In fact, it was such a short time ago you were probably already born.

The weta family loved their tree. There were long, leafy branches to scuttle along and lots of deep, dark cracks and crevasses to snuggle in while they passed the time of day.

"Ah, this is the life!" Auntie Scrunchjaws said as she rocked up and down on her favourite leaf. "We live in a world of such beauty and abundance. The Great Weta Above has provided everything we need." She flicked out to snag a passing bug and scrunched it down happily. "We have nice, leafy branches that keep our snuggle places cool and damp, even in the hottest summers. And we have all the juicy insects we can eat." She looked down at the postman's house through the dappled leaves. "It is a pity about the People, though," she sighed.

Suddenly, the door to the house slammed and the postman's two daughters came running along the path below. Auntie Scrunchjaws sighed again and peered over her leaf at the little girl below, who was climbing onto the swing. Now, Winnie Weta's favourite place in the tree was the long branch that the rope swing was tied to. When the Child-People played on the swing, the branch shook and quivered. It was fun to cling on as everything heaved and swayed.

"You be careful over there," Old Cruncher rasped from his safe spot on the main trunk. "Those Child-People are very, very dangerous."

Up down jiggle shuffle went Winnie on her bouncy branch. This was an especially good shake-up today. Actually, it was almost too good! She had to hold on very tightly indeed.

"Unpredictable and violent, that's what they are," Old Cruncher clacked on. "You remember what happened to your Uncle Grind, don't you, Winnie?"

Winnie Weta did remember, but she wasn't in the mood to listen to that story just then — all about how Uncle Grind had fallen off the branch and down the back of a Child-Person's pants. Poor Uncle Grind had never been the same after that terrifying experience. He had moved from the tree to the old woodpile down the back of the garden. He had a lonely life there now because none of his wives would go with him — they loved the karaka tree too much.

All of a sudden Winnie's branch gave a particularly big shudder and the piece of bark she was on broke away. There she was: hanging on by only one claw — dangling out in space over the purple and yellow flashes of the little Child-Person's T-shirt and jeans swinging below.

"I told you!" rasped Old Cruncher.

Winnie held on as long as she could but her claw lost its grip. She began to fall down, down, down towards the ground.

"Winnie!" screeched Auntie Scrunchjaws.

Winnie wasn't too worried. She had fallen before. The grass had been springy and soft to land on, and it hadn't taken long at all to scuttle back to the bottom of the tree and scrabble back up home.

However, this time Winnie landed on the grass much sooner than she thought she would! And the grass was longer and springier and curlier than she remembered. It was a different colour too — glossy black. She clambered through it, trying to get her bearings so she could run back to the bottom of the tree. But all she could see was the world swishing by, back and forth, back and forth, streaks of green and dappled light.

Suddenly, a huge pink hand, big enough to cover Winnie up three times over, landed in the springy grass next to her. One of the enormous fat fingers poked at her leg. There was a piercing scream and the hand disappeared.

"There's something in my hair!" a voice yelled.

"It's probably a twig," said the other Child-Person. "Get off the swing and let me have a look."

Winnie felt a jolt and looked around her. The world had stopped swinging. Then a huge face loomed over her. The nose alone was bigger than Winnie. She could have fitted easily inside one of the nostrils. And there were two huge round blue eyes. They stared at her in horror. The mouth in the face opened to scream. Winnie found herself looking into a huge wet cavern.

"A weta!!!!" yelled the mouth.

"Get it off! Get it off!" yelled the other voice below the head of hair.

"I can't!" yelled the mouth, "I'm not going to touch it!"

"Flick it off with a stick or something!"

The face with the cave mouth disappeared. "I'll squash it with this!" Winnie heard, and saw a huge block of wood whistling down towards her.

"No!" The head Winnie was on ducked out of the way. "You'll mush it into my hair! Get Mummy! Mummy! Mummy!"

Winnie found herself moving along again. The post-man's house jolted past as Winnie clung on. She thought of jabbing her ovipositor in for a better grip but was afraid that would make the Child-Person run even faster.

They bobbed along the path beside the grapevine towards the front door. Winnie saw her chance. She bent her back legs and sprang up with all her strength. Up and out and over . . . and onto a curling green wisp of grapevine. The wailing voice and thundering footsteps became muffled

148

as they disappeared into the house.

"What on earth's the matter?"

"It's a weta in my hair, Mummy! Get it out!"

"But there's nothing there, dear."

Winnie scrambled along the vine then leapt down onto the path. She landed rather heavily, gave herself a shake then scuttled as fast as her six legs could carry her to the bottom of the tree. She scrambled back up more quickly than you could say "That was a narrow escape".

Old Cruncher clacked his jaw crossly. "That was a narrow escape! I hope it taught you a lesson, young weta!"

"Yes," said Auntie Scrunchjaws, "You won't be going back up on that branch again, I hope!"

But, after a few moments to catch her breath, Winnie headed back to her favourite spot.

"I'm not letting those Child-People keep me away from my favourite branch," she thought as she snuggled against the lovely rough bark. "Anyway," she smiled a little weta smile, "they are far more scared of me than I am of them!"

30

Scimitar Claws!

Jennifer Maxwell

"Can I help you?" shouted Gemma, who couldn't see over the top of the high bakery counter.

Iris Wagtail peered through the glass doors of the pie warmer. "I'll have *that* one please," she said — but she was pointing at Gemma.

"To eat here or take away?" said Gemma's mother.

"To take away," said Iris. "I think it would make a good dog handler."

"I'm a baker's assistant," said Gemma. "Not a dog handler."

"But you're very good with Daisybelle," said Iris. "Please hurry up."

Gemma hurried. She liked Iris Wagtail's small, square dog. "Daisybelle is square, not round," Iris would say if anyone mentioned her shape. "She is short for her size. She is big-boned. Like me."

Iris was a painter, although a good deal of her paint

ended up in her hair and on her small, square dog. Today Iris had bright, buttercup streaks in her ponytail and Daisybelle had a matching buttercup ear.

"Cadmium yellow," said Iris. "Isn't it gorgeous? Come along."

"Where are we going?"

"To Mr Shuttlecock's Exclusive Holiday Hotel. He has an unwanted visitor."

"Who?" said Gemma.

"Not *who*," said Iris, "but *what*. A wild animal. Possibly a possum. Mr Shuttlecock has searched the hotel from top to bottom but he can't find it."

"Then how does he know it's there?"

"Because it leaves its spoor all over the floors."

"Yuk," said Gemma.

"*Spoor*," said Iris, "is not just a wild animal's droppings. It is its smell and its footprints. And Daisybelle is going to track it down."

They both looked down at Daisybelle. Gemma said nothing.

"I know what you're thinking," said Iris sternly. "But hunting is in Daisybelle's blood. Long ago, dogs like her were the only ones who could search out the small, square lairs of the razor-toothed, scimitar-clawed . . ." Iris leaned down and whispered something in Gemma's ear.

"What's a ba — " began Gemma.

"Don't! Don't say that word aloud in front of Daisybelle. Not unless it's an emergency."

"Exclusive Guests," said Mr Shuttlecock. "I have asked you

here to meet Daisybelle, who has kindly offered to track down our unwanted visitor."

Daisybelle lay on her back in the living room of Mr Shuttlecock's Exclusive Holiday Hotel, and invited the guests to tickle her tummy.

"Where I come from," observed the lady from Alabama, "the hound dogs are a mite taller."

"And where I come from," said the sheep farmer from Australia, "they're a darn sight thinner."

"Where I come from," said the accountant from Auckland, "the dogs are trained professionals."

(The man from Oman said nothing at all as he didn't know what they were talking about, and the honeymooners from Japan giggled behind their hands.)

"Taller?" said Iris Wagtail. "*Thinner? Professional? Gemma,*" she said, "this is an emergency."

Gemma knelt down and whispered *the word* into Daisybelle's cadmium-yellow ear.

Daisybelle sat up. She stared at Gemma as if she was trying to remember where she'd buried her favourite bone. Then, deep within her eyes Gemma glimpsed something terrible — short and square, a razor-toothed, scimitar-clawed . . .

"... *badger!*" said Gemma out loud.

Daisybelle stood up. She scented the air. She lowered her nose to the carpet and sniffed long and loud.

Then she took off! A small, square, black, white and yellow blur that streaked between the jandalled feet of the accountant from Auckland and ruffled the long dishdasha of the man from Oman. She raced beneath the billiard table, nose to the ground, a stray billiard ball bouncing ahead of her. She skated across the lobby with her nose in the air, into the cloakroom, startling the gumboots into piles and scaring the umbrellas right out of their stands. She hurtled across the kitchen, skidding on the linoleum and slurping up crumbs on the run, she scooted under the boxes in the hall cupboard, making them buck and bounce, she tore down the hallway to the bottom of the stairs . . .

"Follow that dog!" shouted the sheep farmer from Australia.

They charged up the stairs after Daisybelle — Gemma and Iris and Mr Shuttlecock, the sheep farmer from Australia, the lady from Alabama, the accountant from Auckland, the man from Oman with his dishdasha swirling — and, arm in arm in the rear, the honeymooners from Japan.

Daisybelle darted under the beds, ploughing up dustballs with her nose. She dived into the bathrooms and chased the soap around the showers. She dashed into the sitting room . . .

. . . and stopped.

They all stopped.

Daisybelle stared very hard at a small, square settee.

"There's nothing here," panted Mr Shuttlecock. "I've checked this room three times."

Daisybelle let out a howl.

Ear-splitting! Blood-curdling! Eye-boggling and knee-wobbling!

She plunged into the small, square space beneath the settee, flipped onto her back, and scrabbled and paddled until she disappeared.

Very carefully, Mr Shuttlecock and Iris Wagtail raised the settee. Gemma got down and looked beneath it.

Nothing.

Nothing but Daisybelle, growling and howling, gripping and snarling and shaking her head ferociously from side to side until . . .

Rrrrr . . . ip!

"Oh my stars and garters!" said the lady from Alabama.

"Well, stone the crows," said the sheep farmer from Australia.

"A hedgehog!" said Mr Shuttlecock. "Nesting in my upholstery. I would never have found it without Daisybelle."

"That dog knows its business," agreed the accountant from Auckland.

The guests took photographs of Daisybelle and Gemma

and the hedgehog to show to their families back home. The man from Oman tickled Daisybelle's tummy, the honeymooners from Japan bowed respectfully and Mr Shuttlecock gave her a great big bone.

"It wasn't as big as a you-know-what," said Iris as they shared leftover éclairs at the bakery.

"Or a possum," said Gemma.

"But it *was* a very large hedgehog," said Iris, "for its size."

"Big-boned," said Gemma.

"Prickles like darning needles."

"And did you see those *claws*?" said Gemma.

Acknowledgements

The publisher gratefully acknowledges the following authors and publishers for permission to reproduce the stories. Where there is no publishing credit, the story is previously unpublished and all rights remain with the authors.

'The Korimako Kid', © Rachel Hayward

'Harry', © Margaret Beames

'Cat Attack', © Maria Gill

'Marry a Rat', © Lorraine Williams, first published in *School Journal*, part 3, no. 2, 1980 (reworked).

'The Little Koura', © Debra Smallholme

'The Biggest Liar and Thief I've Ever Met', © Jack Lasenby, first published in *Harry Wakatipu*, McIndoe, 1993.

'The Giant Weta Detective Agency', © James Norcliffe

'Tui and the Pony', © Jane Buxton, first published in *School Journal*, part 2, no. 4, 1989.

'Pass It On', © David Hill

'Wild Tiger', © Bill Nagelkerke

'Henny Penny', © Janice Leitch

'Dinosaurs at the Deluxe Dog Motel', © Peter Friend

'Wool You Join Us?', © David Hill

'Charley Two', © Lorraine Orman

'Bone Growing', © Janice Marriott

'Don't Feed the Keas', © Darlene Thomson

'The Weta in the Letterbox', © Wanda Cowley

'Bonecrusher', © Janice Leitch

'Mad About Elephants', © Margaret Beames

'Chirpy', © John Parker, first published in *School Journal*, part 3, no 1, 2000.

'The Rat and the Little Black Scaup', © James Norcliffe

'Fair Shares', © David Hill

'The Scribbily Scrabbily Dinosaur', © Alan Bagnall

'The Butterfly', © Dianne Hogan

157

Index of Stories by Author

Bagnall, Alan, 'The Scribbily Scrabbily Dinosaur' 118

Beames, Margaret, 'Harry' 20

   'Mad About Elephants' 99

Buxton, Jane, 'The Last Horses' 126

   'Tui and the Pony' 48

Cowley, Wanda, 'The Weta in the Letterbox' 90

Else, Barbara, 'Ms Winsley and the Incognito TV Star' 130

Friend, Peter, 'Dinosaurs at the Deluxe Dog Motel' 66

Gill, Maria, 'Cat Attack' 25

   'Operation "Dog"' 136

Hayward, Rachel, 'A Tail in the Chimney' 139

   'The Korimako Kid' 13

Hill, David, 'Fair Shares' 113

   'Pass It On' 54

   'Wool You Join Us?' 72

Hogan, Dianne, 'The Butterfly' 121

Lasenby, Jack, 'The Biggest Liar and Thief I've Ever Met' 36

Leitch, Janice, 'Bonecrusher' 94

   'Henny Penny' 62

Marriott, Janice, 'Bone Growing' 81

Maxwell, Jennifer, 'Scimitar Claws!' 150

Nagelkerke, Bill, 'Wild Tiger' 58

Norcliffe, James, 'The Giant Weta Detective Agency' 43

   'The Rat and the Little Black Scaup' 108

Orman, Lorraine, 'Charley Two' 76

Parker, John, 'Chirpy' 104

Smallholme, Debra, 'The Little Koura' 31

Thomson, Darlene, 'Don't Feed the Keas' 86

Thorburn, Jan, 'Winnie Weta's Scary Adventure with
   the Child-People' 145

Williams, Lorraine, 'Marry a Rat' 27